Bicycling Books®

BEST
BICYCLE TOURS
VOLUME 2

*by the editors of **Bicycling**®magazine*

Cover photograph by Sally Ann Shenk
Book series design by K. A. Schell
Layout by Jeanne Stock
Illustrations by David Bullock
Edited by Kathy Fones

Library of Congress Cataloging in Publication Data (Revised)
Main entry under title:

Best bicycle tours.

    (Bicycling books series)
    Includes bibliographical references.
    1. Bicycle touring—United States—Guide-books—
Collected works. 2. Bicycle touring—Canada—Guide-
books—Collected works. 3. Bicycle touring—Germany,
West—Guide-books—Collected works. 4. United States—
Description and travel—1960-   —Guide-books—
Collected works. 5. Canada—Description and travel—
1951-   —Guide-books—Collected works. 6. Germany,
West—Description and travel—Guide-books—Collected
works. I. Bicycling (Emmaus, Pa.) II. Series
GV1045.B43   917.3   80-18355

ISBN 0-87857-336-4 paperback
2 4 6 8 10 9 7 5 3 1 paperback

Contents

We are indebted to the readers of *Bicycling* magazine for their help in providing tour information.

While we have double-checked all route information before going to press, cyclists are advised to obtain detailed maps of the specific touring areas. Cyclists are also advised to be wary of road conditions that could change "overnight." Check with the listed information sources before beginning a tour.

Introduction

If you have a bike and would like to use it for more than cycling around the block, *Best Bicycle Tours* is for you. Why is that so?

Well, take a look at the roads around you. Chances are, they are full of traffic, hardly the place you'd go for a leisurely bicycle ride. Yet with our miles of super highways we tend to forget that there are literally tens-of-thousands of miles of roads in America that are largely traffic-free.

Our sophisticated highway network has reduced our country to a grid for fast travel. Even with a 55 mph speed limit we can get from point A to B in record time. And contemporary life-styles demand such speed.

At the same time our need for leisure—and a space to practice it—is all the more essential these days. So, paradoxically, we owe the highway engineers a debt of gratitude for "driving" cars from so many beautiful miles of American landscape.

In my own touring I've frequently been amazed at the number of gentle lanes and roads within easy distance of a superhighway. In such fashion I've traveled literally for hours without meeting a car.

So to the people who say they won't ride a bike because of the traffic, I say that the backroads of America wait to be discovered. However, if the discovering is to be a pleasurable experience, you will need a reliable roadmap. And that is where *Best Bicycle Tours* comes in.

All of the tours in this book have been road-tested by qualified cyclists. That is, the actual routes have been ridden on a bike by a veteran cyclist who well knows the needs of the bicycle tourist.

The tours themselves are situated in a number of states including Vermont, Massachusetts, New York, Rhode Island, Connecticut, Pennsylvania, New Jersey, Virginia, North Carolina, Florida, Michigan, Texas, Idaho, Utah, Arizona, and California. You should know that although each tour has a specific route and length, individual tours have a hundred variations. And that is the beauty of bicycle travel; you move through an environment at a speed that will allow you to interpret and enjoy. Side roads beckon in a way they don't when you travel by car.

Each tour is presented with the traveler in mind, with good emphasis on route, accommodations, level of difficulty, points of interest, and recommendations about riding.

Furthermore, *Best Bicycle Tours* contains a variety of tours that will appeal to both beginning and more seasoned cyclists. The point is each tour can be interpreted and ridden according to your abilities and needs.

This book would not have been possible without the help of Bonnie Wong and the members of her Touring Exchange who are in the vanguard of exploring new and interesting cycling routes in this country. (To receive copies of Touring Exchange tours, send $1 and a stamped, self-addressed envelope to Touring Exchange, 1320 North Fir Villa Road, Dallas, OR 97338.) Similarly, the readers of *Bicycling* magazine were very helpful in testing and submitting a number of these tours.

We hope you make these tours a part of your holiday and travel plans. And if you have any comments about these tours or have new tours of your own, I'd love to receive them.

James C. McCullagh
Editor/Publisher
Bicycling magazine

Three Routes
in Northern Massachusetts

Tour I: Methuen-Lowell-Dunstable-Groton

Location

This 54.6-mile, one-day loop tour begins and ends in Methuen, Massachusetts. You'll cycle through Lowell, a large northern industrial city enjoying a rebirth in terms of its rich historic past, and through Dunstable and Groton. The route consists of two long sections of very flat road along the Merrimac River, separated by about 20 miles of hills surrounding Groton. You could begin the ride at Lowell University instead, thereby shortening the tour by about 15 miles.

Season

Because this tour travels through some lovely heavily forested areas, it is particularly beautiful to ride in the fall. But the route can be ridden in any season.

Accommodations

Facilities are limited on this ride, so a picnic lunch is recommended. There is a small general store in Groton.

Level of Difficulty

The river road is wide, flat, and smooth. The roads used are lightly traveled so the ride is peaceful and leisurely and can be enjoyed by all cyclists.

References

General highway maps can be obtained from the Massachusetts

3

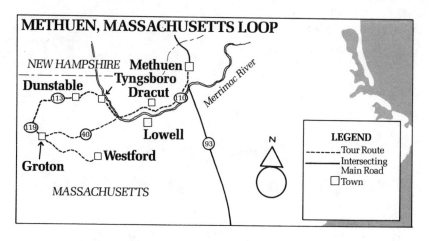

METHUEN, MASSACHUSETTS LOOP

NEW HAMPSHIRE **Methuen**

Dunstable **Tyngsboro**

Dracut

Merrimac River

Lowell

Westford

Groton

MASSACHUSETTS

N

LEGEND
------- Tour Route
——— Intersecting
Main Road
☐ Town

Department of Public Works, 100 Nashua Street, Boston, MA 02114.

Tour Outline and Points of Interest

0.0: Begin at the Texaco station located just off Route 93 at the Route 110 exit. The highway sign will read 110-113 Lawrence, Dracut. Proceed around the rotary until the Texaco self-service gas station comes into view. You will follow Route 110 toward Lowell. This road winds along the historic Merrimac River which at one time fueled a significant portion of the Industrial Revolution in America. The huge mill towns of Manchester, New Hampshire, and Lowell, Lawrence, and Haverhill, Massachusetts, all drew their power from this river.

0.2: On the left you will note the seaplanes which are available to prospective sightseers. You can take a 15-minute flight over the upcoming route to survey the topography.

2.9: The sign indicates that you are now entering Dracut. From the numerous outlooks at the river along this road you will see a greatly purified version of a once heavily polluted river. Various regulations and purification plants have helped cleanse the river in recent years.

7.1: Entering Lowell the predominant feature is the mills lining the opposite side of the river. It is difficult now to journey back 50 years in time and see this as the boom town that it once was. Days could be easily spent exploring the intricate system of canals devised by early engineers to pioneer textile manufacturing in America on a huge scale. The water outlets beneath the mills are still clearly visible. Continue along Route 110.

8.7: Lowell University and its unused nuclear reactor sit on your right.

9.8: Route 110 bears directly into Route 113 here. Continue right along the river on 113.

11.5: The Lowell Community Vegetable Gardens on the right are reminiscent of the victory gardens in Boston's Fenway. On a Sunday morning in autumn many of the multiethnic residents of Lowell will be harvesting their crops.

12.5: The sign says Tyngsboro and you have yet to see a hill. Be patient.

13.9: The wind sock on the right in the middle of a grass field marks the private airstrip of a local flyer. If you're lucky you'll see him bounce in for a landing in his Piper Cub as you ride by.

15.4: The road on which you are riding ends at the large steel span crossing the Merrimac. Stay on Route 110 as it crosses the bridge and continue to follow it.

15.7: Tyngsboro Town Hall is on the left, and you are entering a part of Massachusetts largely unknown to urban residents of the state. This countryside is covered by successful farms. For a mile or so out of Tyngsboro the surface of Route 113 is a bit rough, but it does clear up soon.

17.1: Entering Dunstable.

18.1: A small burying ground on the right marks the final resting place of some of the early settlers of Dunstable. A number of tablets and markers along the route record that many settlers had quite a toussle with the Indians of this area.

19.2: In Dunstable center continue along Route 113.

19.9: Bear left on Groton Street where the sign says Groton 6.

22.7: You'll pass from Dunstable to Groton and a small sign on the roadside marks the occasion.

25.7: Bear right at the burial ground as you enter the town proper of Groton.

25.9: Take a left on Route 119 and continue through Groton.

27.1: Bear left on Route 40 toward Westford and climb the short hills alongside the white clapboard church. You will suffer a few hills in the next miles so be prepared. But the scenery and the farm-land are quite worth the effort.

31.3: M.I.T. Lincoln Labs sit on the left side of the road.

32.8: Continue on Route 40 as it bears left past a small burial yard.

34.3: Take a left turn on Tyngsboro Road and continue along here for four miles. You will end on top of a small hill overlooking the Merrimac River and the bridge over which you originally crossed.

34.6: Recross the steel bridge and return along Route 113 toward

Lowell. This is the simplest, flattest, least trafficked route.

41.2: While again passing through Lowell note the construction at the river dam. In several of the cities along the Merrimac, power plants are now in construction.

54.6: Tired legs get a rest as you return to your start at Route 93.

Tour II: Gloucester-Rockport-Gloucester

Location

The Gloucester-Rockport coastal loop is known to all Boston area cyclists as one of the region's finest, most scenic rides. There is much to see and so many places to stop and explore that the

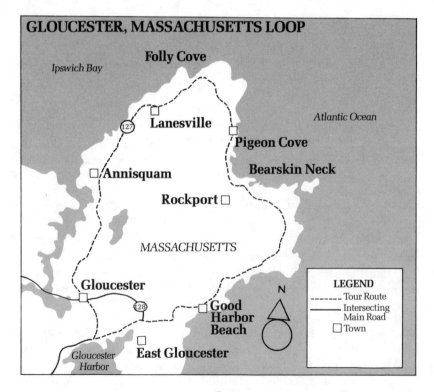

GLOUCESTER, MASSACHUSETTS LOOP

Folly Cove

Ipswich Bay

127 Lanesville

Atlantic Ocean

Pigeon Cove

Annisquam

Bearskin Neck

Rockport

MASSACHUSETTS

Gloucester

128

Good Harbor Beach

N

East Gloucester

Gloucester Harbor

LEGEND
------- Tour Route
——— Intersecting Main Road
☐ Town

indicated 19.8-mile route is easily a day's journey for an inquisitive traveler.

Season

Spring and fall are the ideal times to cycle this tour. The temperature on Cape Ann is well tempered by the cold ocean air and breezes so a sweater is usually necessary. And the Cape Ann beach water is very clear, cold, and refreshing for the tired cyclist.

Accommodations

Restaurants are plentiful and the seafood is superb, so unless a picnic is planned, food need not be carried. There are no bike shops on most of the route, so check your bike over before you begin.

Level of Difficulty

The roads may be narrow and winding in some places, but they are all in good condition. The main problem here is a steady flow of traffic at busy times. Rockport is a hectic tourist attraction so beware of Sunday afternoons during the summer. Plan to cycle on weekdays if possible.

References

General highway maps can be obtained from the Massachusetts Department of Public Works, 100 Nashua Street, Boston, MA 02114.

Tour Outline and Points of Interest

0.0: The ride begins at Gloucester Harbor and its well known statue of the fisherman at the wheel of his ship. From the feet of the fisherman you can watch the small trawlers that carry the Portuguese sailors out to Georges Bank and their work. If you plan ahead you will hit the Sunday in June when the Blessing of the Fleet takes place. This religious festival abounds in good food and always attracts a crowd of people both participating in the Blessing and enjoying the food and spirit of celebration.

1.4: If you've managed to find your way out of the city you will be proceeding out Route 127 to the road to East Gloucester that bears to the right. This takes you by many fish canneries, parts of the fishing fleet at rest, and the beginnings of a new arts and crafts colony in East Gloucester.

4.1: On the outer side of Eastern Point you'll pass a long uninterrupted portion of Atlantic beaches and rocky shore. If the sea is rough you will begin to better appreciate the fish luncheon that you may enjoy somewhere down the road knowing some of the danger faced by the fishermen who landed the catch.

5.7: At the end of Eastern Point you will cross a small bridge with Good Harbor Beach way out to the right over the wide salt marshes. It is worthwhile to note these marshes and the many others scattered along this route because of the critical role they play in preventing flood and ocean damage in the winter storms. The marsh zone prevents excessive water buildup and speeds drainage while open beaches and rocky shore often suffer remarkable damage.

6.8: Bear left at the sign to Rockport.

10.1: Bearskin Neck is a well-developed arts colony awash with tourists. It is a charming center and the off-season allows better enjoyment of its offerings. Motif #1#2 (the original was destroyed in the blizzard of 1978) can be seen and a variety of lobster and pleasure boats always grace the moorings. There are several worthy lunch stops here, and if you like crafts, this is the place.

10.4: Still on Route 127 you now pass the Rockport Tool Company. On a hot day the doors are opened and in the fiery glow of forges and furnaces worked by people with smoke-blackened faces you are reminded of what it would be like visiting a 19th century Welsh coal works. It is a rather remarkable image.

A right turn immediately after the tool works will allow a quick visit to the neat little harbor at Pigeon Cove. Notice the care taken in construction of the granite breakwater. It is well to note that in the early days these huge granite blocks were broken off using hand drills and raw muscle. In our mechanized age it is remarkable to think of the days when 20-ton blocks were handcut and moved by horse-drawn winches.

13.3: Folly Cove is the small bay on the right which next catches your interest. It is fair game now for skindivers and lobster traps, although its name suggests the dearth of wisdom shown by anyone trying to wait out a northeast storm in its lee. There is no lee and the huge northeasterly rollers break right on its rocky beach.

13.4: A quick tour through the town cemetery will point out the various colored stones marking the graves of early stonecutters. It was a common practice for Norwegian and Finnish emigrants to bring with them stones from the old country to mark their final resting places. Note also the stairway cut into the huge granite boulder near the cemetery entrance.

14.3: At the small Sauna sign, bear right to Lanes Cove. This tiny harbor sports its own fleet and would be a delightful place to have lunch. Explore it carefully and make sure you find the small, shaded cemetery up on the left overlooking the water. In it are buried most of Lanesville's earliest residents.

15.7: After Lanesville you will be riding along Ipswich Bay until you reach Annisquam. This small neck is worthy of a pass through as it sports a number of well-built old homes which bear the careful marks of the shipwrights who built them.

18.6: Carefully go around the Route 128 rotary and continue on Route 127 toward Gloucester.

19.8: After winding your way through the city of Gloucester you will find yourself back at the point of departure, the statue of the fisherman.

Tour III: Beverly-Magnolia-Essex-Wenham

Location

This 33.9-mile ride passes through the seat of some of the oldest wealth in the United States. As you wind your way through Beverly, Beverly Farms, Manchester, Gloucester, Essex, and Wenham, you will pass some remarkable estates, many of which date back to well before the birth of the Republic. It's a remarkably pleasant route.

Season

This ride can be taken any time of year. The North Shore's cold

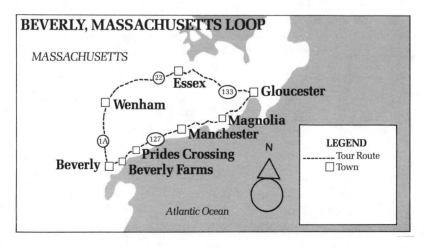

BEVERLY, MASSACHUSETTS LOOP

MASSACHUSETTS

Essex
Gloucester
Wenham
Magnolia
Manchester
Beverly
Prides Crossing
Beverly Farms

N

LEGEND
------- Tour Route
☐ Town

Atlantic Ocean

9

water usually cools off the coast road on all but the hottest days, and sometimes produces a head wind. So be prepared for cool breezy weather along this route, no matter what time of year.

Accommodations

Points of interest and eating places are plentiful so it is not necessary to carry food, especially since Essex is world renowned for its clams.

Level of Difficulty

Terrain is moderate, roads are smooth and well surfaced, shoulders are wide, and traffic is not too bad.

References

General highway maps can be obtained from the Massachusetts Department of Public Works, 100 Nashua Street, Boston, MA 02114.

Tour Outline and Points of Interest

0.0: Leave Beverly at the intersection of Route 127 and Main Street. This is just up the road from the McDonald's on Route 1A. Immediately bearing right on Route 127, start on your way.

0.4: On the right there is a small park but it's too early to rest so push on. The Salem Willows Park is directly across the water from here.

0.8: Mackerel Cove Beach lies to the right. Many of the North Shore's beaches are all but inaccessible to any but resident autos during the season. But if you get the urge to leave your bike and go for a dip, bikes are welcome almost anywhere. Don't panic though because there are still a number of fine beaches on this route.

2.6: You'll pass on the right a small cove that marks the entry to Beverly Farms. This section of road boasts (quietly) some of the North Shore's most stately mansions.

3.6: Prides Crossing marks this point on the ride and a small country store will provide snacks or drinks. Prides Crossing is a stop on the B & M and an easy train ride from Boston's North Station.

5.8: Harbor Street on the right marks a short but interesting detour to check out a lovely beach and the Manchester Yacht Club. At the end of Harbor Street (about ⅛ mile down) a right will take you to a tiny, little-known beach and a left to the yacht club. You may note the rather well known name of Cabot on the property straight across Harbor Street.

7.2: You are now back on Route 127 and continuing your tour.

7.9: Bear right on Central Street toward Manchester by the Sea, and in another $1/10$ mile you'll come to the center of Manchester.

8.0: After Manchester continue straight ahead where Route 127 forks to the left and proceed toward Singing Beach.

8.6: Singing Beach is a fine ocean beach. On a hot summer day you will find the water very refreshing. In the early spring or later in the fall the swells can be quite large here. A lack of available parking does an excellent job of crowd control. From here you'll reverse direction and head back toward Manchester.

9.3: Turn right on Route 127 and continue toward Magnolia.

9.5: An old cemetery is found on the side of the road. A quick walk through can shed more than a little light on the lives of the pioneers who first lived in the community. Pioneer life was not always the romantic, fulfilling dream that we now envision.

12.0: Bear right onto the road to Magnolia.

12.5: In Magnolia center quickly bear right onto Shore Road. This road is rough and narrow but has relatively little traffic and is well worth the few bumps you will encounter. A fine piece of rocky New England shore lies at the end of the road.

13.1: At the end of Shore Road take a left and shortly after a right onto Lexington Avenue. Here you'll pass through the Magnolia shopping district. At the end of Lexington Avenue take a right and continue on this road.

14.3: Hammond Castle is a North Shore oddity on the right-hand side. Built by an early millionaire who made his fortune in South African diamonds, it is held in high esteem for the quality of its organ and performance hall. It is an interesting place and well worth the visit.

14.9: Bear right at the end of this road. You are now back on Route 127 and Gloucester bound.

16.2: Gliding down a long hill you enter Gloucester with its large, well-known harbor on the right. Spend some time cruising along the walk, take a few pictures of the fishermen and then head to Route 133 toward Essex.

19.2: The road to Essex is quiet, smooth, and relatively uneventful. Essex itself is a rather peaceful little town which has gained no small reputation as a clam and seafood center. It may be worthwhile to scout around a bit and have lunch here, if you've passed up the three or four previous lunch stops.

22.7: Take a left into Essex Center onto Route 22.

26.5: Continue straight on Larch Road. Route 22 turns sharply (though unmarked) left here and will go back to Beverly, but Larch Road is a bit quieter.

27.6: You'll pass Myopia Hunt Club. On a fine fall day you may see groups of horsemen galloping off into the sunset. Myopia is the hub of the North Shore horse set.

29.1: At the end of Larch Road take a left on Route 1A. You are now in Wenham. Follow 1A for 4.8 miles right into Beverly and back to Route 127 and the start.

Notes

Three Tours in Vermont

Location

Vermont is a bicycle tourist's paradise: miles upon miles of gentle country roads, the beauty of the Green Mountains, quaint country inns that cater to bicycle tourists, and an excellent state park system. Here are two enjoyable tours in Vermont, one centered around Middlebury, the other around Bennington, plus an optional tour connecting the two towns.

Both Middlebury and Bennington are serviced by Greyhound and Trailways bus lines. The closest Vermont airport is in Burlington, about 30 miles from Middlebury. Air New England, U.S. Air, and Delta Airlines have flights into that airport. Amtrak stations are located at Burlington, Montpelier (about 50 miles from Middlebury), and points in-between.

Season

May and June are perhaps the ideal months for cycling in Vermont. Temperatures are mild, roads generally free of traffic, and the countryside alive with wildflowers. Summer is also pleasant; perfect for those who like to take a short break for swimming as temperatures average in the low 80s. Although fall is probably the most spectacular season to tour Vermont, the traffic is the heaviest and the weather the most unpredictable.

Accommodations

Camping is a pleasure in Vermont's excellent state park system. But if you are so inclined to stay in hotels or motels, Middlebury and Bennington both offer a wide selection from which to choose.

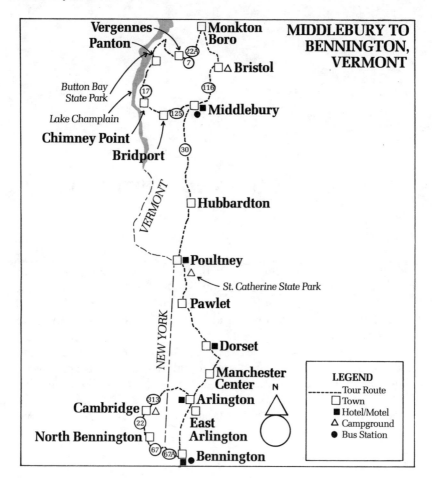

Level of Difficulty

Vermont's terrain is hilly. But with adequate gearing, you can handle all hills. Vermont roads are kept remarkably clean by the well-known bottle bill, which imposes a minimum five-cent deposit on all beverage containers. Another piece of legislation outlaws all billboards. In their place are standardized signs about three by four feet that offer the item of interest, mileage to that point, and a directional arrow.

References

Vermont Agency of Development and Community Affairs, 61 Elm St., Montpelier, VT 05602, Phone (802) 828-3236; Vermont Recreation and Park Association, c/o Recreation Section, Dept. of Forests, Parks and Recreation, Agency of Environmental Conservation, Montpelier, VT 05602; *Vermont: A Guide to the Green Mountain State,* edited by Ray Bearse (3rd ed., 1968); *The Vermont Atlas and Gazetteer,* edited by William Hancock et al. (1978); *The Big Green Book: A Four-Season Guide to Vermont,* by Madeleine Kunin and Marilyn Stout (1976); *Vermont Life,* 61 Elm St., Montpelier, VT 05602; "Vermont—A State of Mind and Mountains," by Ethel A. Starbird, *National Geographic,* July 1974, pp. 28-61.

Tour Outline and Points of Interest

Tour I—Middlebury: This first tour begins and ends in the quaint college town of Middlebury. On this 66-mile route you explore the historic Champlain Valley while traversing rolling farmland, the shores of Lake Champlain, and valley land of the Green Mountains. The scenery is varied, and history buffs can visit sites related to several important battles of the Revolution and War of 1812. I rode this tour in two days, camping at Button Bay State Park. The only negative factor was the wind, which I had to fight a lot along the mountains. Someone told me that whatever way the wind is blowing between Middlebury and Bennington, there always seems to be a head wind for the cyclist.

0.0: Begin in Middlebury. Follow Route 125 west toward Bridport. Two attractions to see are the Frog Hollow Craft Center, the state's first, and the Sheldon Museum, the oldest incorporated town museum in the nation. There are also two bicycle shops here, the Bike & Ski Touring Center, 22 Main Street, Phone (802) 388-6666; and Skihaus Mountain Sports, 56 Main Street, Phone (802) 388-2823.

8.0: Turn right at the stop sign in Bridport to continue west on Route 125. There is a grocery store at this intersection and a larger one just down the road.

8.5: Turn left at Pratt's Store with BP gas pumps (on the left) to stay on Route 125 west to Chimney Point.

15.5: Turn right at Chimney Point onto Route 17 east. Here you'll find an historic site and museum. Just before D.A.R. State Park (on the left) is a 19th century gravestone with faded lettering (on the right). The John Strong D.A.R. Mansion (on the left) is just down from the park.

17.5: Bear left onto Lake Street at Franklin's Country Store with Amoco gas pumps (on the right).

23.5: Turn right onto Pease Road.

24.3: Turn left onto Jersey Street. Use caution in making this

15

turn, which comes suddenly as you ride downhill. And watch for sand littering the road.

24.9: Go straight at the intersection in Panton so you pass Daigneault's Store with Gulf gas pumps (on the left).

25.4: Bear left at the fork onto Sherman Road, which turns into Button Bay Road. Button Bay State Park (on the left) comes after a mile and a half.

28.4: Turn right at the T onto Basin Harbor Road. In about two miles you pass through a 1,000-acre marsh that serves as a refuge for migrating waterfowl.

32.7: Turn left at the stop sign onto the unsigned road.

34.0: Turn left at the stop sign onto West Main Street, which is Route 22A north, to enter Vergennes, where there are grocery stores. Painter's Tavern at the corner of the village green serves excellent lunches and dinners. Other attractions: the Bixby Library Museum; Kennedy Bros., Inc. gift shop (open seven days a week) and woodenware factory (visible from the gift shop, open Monday through Friday); the Rokeby Historical House and waterfalls and boat landing where Macdonough built his ships to defeat the British on Lake Champlain in the War of 1812.

Pedal through the town square and go about ¼ mile. Turn right at the Texaco gas station onto Monkton Road. Go another ¼ mile to the intersection of Monkton Road and Route 7. Go straight through onto Monkton Road.

42.0: Town of Monkton Boro. Grocery.

44.0: Turn right at stop sign in Monkton Ridge onto unsigned road (see sign for Bristol).

50.0: Veer left onto unsigned road marked by sign for Bristol.

52.0: Turn right in Bristol onto West Street.

53.0: Turn left onto Route 116 south. About three miles south of here is Elephant Mountain Camping Area (on the left), R.D. 2, Box 113A, Bristol, VT 05443. Open all year.

62.0: Turn right at Case Street Community Club (old white building with bell and sign, on the left) onto Quarry Road.

65.8: Bear left at stop sign onto Washington Street and ride into Middlebury.

Tour II—Middlebury to Bennington: For those who would like to bicycle from Middlebury to Bennington, this route provides a pleasant 84-mile ride comfortably done in two days. That's how long it took me. A good overnight after 36 miles is St. Catherine State Park just south of Poultney. This ride is quite scenic, passing by several lakes and the ridges of the Green Mountains. And a number of historical attractions dot the route, including a fine museum.

As in the last leg of the Middlebury tour, a strong wind makes its presence known, although after Poultney it died down significantly for me. The terrain is moderate to Hubbardton, with two long uphills. After that the terrain is easy to moderate. One very long uphill I remember in this last part is on the five miles of gravel. The rest of the route is blacktop in good condition. It is also narrow and has little or no shoulder, but the light traffic makes this unimportant.

0.0: Follow Route 30 south out of Middlebury.

20.0: Town of Hubbardton. Grocery.

21.0: Lake Bomoseen Campground (on the right), Bomoseen, VT 05732. Phone (802) 273-2061. Open May 1 through October 15. Other campsites in this immediate area are Lake Bomoseen Recreation Area and Half Moon Pond Recreation Area.

26.0: Swimming at Crystal Beach (on the right). Also at this point is Ringquist's Dining Room, Route 30, Bomoseen, VT 05732. Phone (802) 468-5172.

33.0: Town of Poultney. Highland Gray Inn and Green Mountain College.

36.0: St. Catherine State Park (on the right).

47.0: Town of Pawlet. Good ice cream at The Station Restaurant, 75 yards along a side road west of Route 30.

55.0: Town of Dorset. Lodging at the Dorset Inn, Dorset, VT 05251. Phone (802) 867-5500 or 867-9392. Summer theater (July through September) at the Dorset Playhouse. Good swimming at the old marble quarry.

61.0: Town of Manchester center. The Bicycle Shop, Route 11 and 30. Phone (802) 362-1625.

62.0: Town of Manchester. Go about ¼ mile past the square and turn left at River Road. Colored gray on the state map, this road has five miles of gravel. Follow it to Bennington. Southern Vermont Art Center is just northwest of Manchester. Lunch is served from 11:30 A.M. to 3 P.M. at its Garden Cafe. Reservations are advised; call (802) 362-1405.

71.0: Town of East Arlington. Deceased artist Norman Rockwell lived in nearby Arlington for many years. Grocery in Arlington. Go over bridge and bear left onto Pleasant Street. Ride one block and turn right onto Ice Pond Road. After ⅛ mile turn left at stop sign onto Warm Brook Road (unmarked). Go ¼ mile and turn left onto Maple Hill Road; see sign for the Peter Matteson Tavern (a museum).

74.3: Bear left at the fork to stay on Maple Hill Road. In about a mile you come to the tavern.

84.3: Town of Bennington.

Tour III—Bennington: This third tour carries the bicyclist over 50 miles of easy terrain, starting and ending in historic Bennington. Bennington, one of the largest and busiest towns in Vermont, holds special interest for students of history. Near here, in New York State, General John Stark and his American forces won an important battle by defeating a British invasion force on August 16, 1777. Easy riding allows time for the associated historical attractions as well as enjoyment of some beautiful mountain scenery on the New York side. It is a very easy two-day tour. I rode it in one short day without my touring equipment. Paved all the way, the route uses roads of good surface that are generally narrow but have light traffic.

0.0: Begin in Bennington. Head north on old Route 7 from the intersection of South and Main Streets. Bennington Battle Monument and the Bennington Museum. Other attractions in the greater Bennington area are listed on a map available at the First Vermont Bank at 500 Main Street in Bennington. Two bike shops: Giard's Bike Shop, 208 North Street, Phone (802) 442-3444; and Up and Downhill, Inc., 160 Ben Mont Avenue, Phone (802) 442-8664.

14.0: Town of Arlington. Go through town and turn left at the cemetery onto Route 313. The Arlington Chamber of Commerce, Arlington, VT 05250, publishes a brochure listing things to do and see, motels and restaurants, and other information for travelers.

22.0: Baker's Country Campground, Cambridge, NY 12816 (on the right). Open spring to fall.

31.0: Town of Cambridge. On your right, as you come into town, is The Corner Store. It has good fresh sandwiches. Another recommended eating place is King's bakery. Go straight through town and turn left at stop sign onto Route 22 south.

36.0: Bear left onto Route 67 east.

47.0: Town of North Bennington. Bennington College and the Park-McCullough House. Go through town and turn right at the stop sign onto Route 67A south to Bennington.

50.0: Town of Bennington.

Notes

A Bike 'n Boat Trip from Long Island, New York, to Rhode Island

Location

At a minimum expense you can cover a lot of territory by combining two forms of transportation into one vacation. This is a bike and boat trip from Long Island, New York to Providence, Rhode Island. You can cover long distances, avoid major urban areas, get away from using a car, and utilize two enjoyable means of transportation. All in all, this route covers approximately 150 miles by bike and 100 miles by boat, lasting about two weeks.

Season

Due to the schedules of the ferries utilized in this tour, the only accessible season for the trip is summer.

Accommodations

Lodging is the most expensive part of this trip. To save a considerable amount of money, you might try camping. Reservations for overnight accommodations are essential on Block Island. Farm stands and lunch stands provide refreshing breaks along the entire route.

Level of Difficulty

The majority of this tour is blessed with flat terrain which makes for easy biking. The route meanders through quaint hamlets and villages separated by vast stretches of bountiful farmlands. It can be ridden by even a beginner bicycle tourist in the two-week time span.

References

For maps and background information, write to the Chambers

of Commerce of the towns and cities on the tour. For current ferry schedules and fares write: Cross Sound Ferry, Box 33, New London, CT 06320; Nelseco Navigation Co., P.O. Box 482, New London, CT 06320.

Tour Outline and Points of Interest

Beginning in East Moriches, Long Island, use Route 27A, locally known as the Montauk Highway or, in parts, Main Street. It's an excellent, often tree-lined, bike route with wide road shoulders, meandering through small towns. 27A becomes 27, then turn onto 79 to Sag Harbor.

Orient Point, at the extreme northeastern tip of Long Island, is the first destination. After biking through the 19th century whaling village of Sag Harbor, Long Island, take the Shelter Island and Greenport Ferry for a 10-minute trip over the South Shore of Shelter Island. It's no more than five miles across Shelter Island along Route 114. Then, another 10-minute ferry ride from Shelter Island over to Greenport, on Long Island's historic North Fork. Ferry service to and from Shelter Island is frequent and the rate is a mere 75¢ each way.

Don't plan on staying in Orient overnight. The State Park has no camping facilities. Your best bet is to stay either in Greenport or East Marion where guesthouses and motels are more available. Because I wanted to get the 7 A.M. ferry out of Orient Point the next morning, I stayed in the only hotel in Orient, The Bay House. It's a rambling, three-story, turn-of-the-century, frame boarding house which time and traffic has left behind. The Bay House is located about ¼ mile south of Route 25 on Main Street overlooking Peconic Bay in the village of Orient. This is about four miles west of Orient Point.

Orient, like Shelter Island, is perfect and picturesque for biking. For an excellent, fresh, and reasonable seafood dinner, try a restaurant called Orient-by-the-Sea on Route 25 just before the ferry terminus in Orient Point. There are no restaurants in Orient, another factor which makes East Marion and Greenport more attractive overnight destinations.

Biking along the North Fork's Route 25, old milestones can be noticed in place along the roadside pointing the distance to "Suffolk C.H." (meaning Suffolk Court House or Riverhead, the county seat).

Another thing about Long Island's North Fork—it has to be one of the few places in the world where helicopters can wake you up at 5:30 A.M. as they're spraying the local potato fields in the predawn stillness.

Flat, open roads, sweeping vistas of farms, potato fields, old

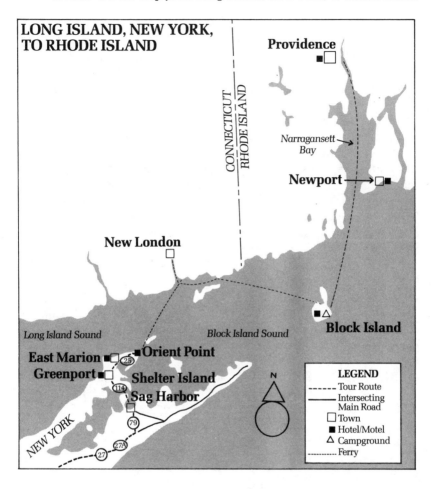

homesteads, Long Island Sound, and Peconic Bay, combined with beautiful summer biking weather, make a memorable visit to eastern Long Island.

The Orient Point-New London Ferry crosses Long Island Sound. Sailing time is one hour, 20 minutes. The charge is $3 one way, bike included. There is frequent ferry service especially during the summer months. Advance reservations for bikers are not necessary and there are no lines or delays getting bikes on board. It's usually a beautiful sail during which you can walk the decks, visit the snack bar on board, or sunbathe up on the top deck. Plan ahead and bring your own meal on board.

In New London, take the ferry that runs between here and Block

Island, a sea distance of 28 miles. This is a summer-only ferry line that leaves New London for Block Island only once a day at 10:30 A.M. with extra trips at 7 P.M. on Fridays. Adult fare, one way, is $5.75 plus $1.50 per bike. The sailing time from New London to Block Island is about two hours, 45 minutes. The ferry itself is a good-sized steamer. A tip: bring your own lunch aboard. Long lines and mediocre food mar the service of the ferry.

Block Island caters to bike fans. It's a family-oriented island, three miles wide and seven miles long. It has about 500 year-round residents and thousands of summer visitors. Many low hills, good road surfaces, and Victorian architecture predominate. Block Island is about 12 miles off the coast of Rhode Island. Many interesting historical markers, long sandy beaches, numerous inns, and guesthouses dot the island. Just about everyplace makes provisions for your bike.

After disembarking in New Harbor, Block Island, bike across to Old Harbor, a distance of not more than a mile or so. Old Harbor is most interesting and popular; it's on the Atlantic Ocean. One of the first things you should do is purchase a map of the island which is available almost everywhere for 10¢. Advance reservations for accommodations are almost essential. You can get a listing of hotels and guesthouses from the Chamber of Commerce, Block Island 02807. I stayed at the Gables Inn located in the center of Old Harbor (Box 516, Dodge St., Block Island 02807) where the proprietors make you feel truly at home. Rates run about $25 daily for two persons; $145 weekly, in a room with a shared bath. On Block Island, a room with a private bath is not only rare but also double the rate. Inns and guesthouses always make provisions for storing your bike overnight.

Needless to say, excellent seafood restaurants abound on Block Island. The local residents go out of their way to be friendly, helpful, and hospitable. People always seem to congregate on the dock at both Old and New Harbor to watch the ferries come and go.

Another excellent hotel on Block Island is the Surf Hotel located right on the main street of Old Harbor. It is characterized by truly Victorian architecture. The house has a rambling wrap-around porch lined with rocking chairs, a huge yet cozy dining room, popcorn sold on the front porch from a turn-of-the-century pushcart, a front lobby in super-Victorian mint condition, the old tin roof, parlor chairs, and bookcases that are overflowing. All combined, it creates a warm and elegant atmosphere.

Take "The Yankee," a summer-only ferry that connects Block Island with both Newport and Providence. A steamer built in 1907, "The Yankee" plies the waters under the command of affable Captain

Michael Smith in the pilothouse. One way, Block Island–Newport, is $3.75, plus $1.25 for your bike.

One way, Newport–Providence, is $2.50, plus $1.25 for your bike.

Of course, it's great to have a bike in Newport. The Mansions, Cliff Walk, and Ocean Drive, all lend themselves to leisurely bike tours. Much of Newport's waterfront area has been revitalized and is now a prime tourist magnet. Restored colonial homes, beautiful Narragansett Bay, superior craft shops and restaurants, sweeping beaches, the Tennis Hall of Fame, the U.S. Naval Base, these and so much more attract bikers and nonbikers to Newport. Write ahead to the Chamber of Commerce, Newport, RI 02840, for a listing of places to stay.

As already noted, "The Yankee" steams between Newport and Providence. As you leave Newport and sail north in Narragansett Bay, you pass beneath the monumental Newport Bridge and then are treated to a memorable view of the U.S. Naval Base in Newport. As the bay narrows into the Seekonk River, the skyline of Providence appears ahead. Providence is the capital of Rhode Island and New England's second largest city.

Notes

Massachusetts to North Carolina

Location

Hanover, Massachusetts, is the starting point for this east coast tour, and can be reached by flying to Logan Airport and taking any of the bus terminals from Boston south to Hanover, about 20 to 25 miles (South Shore). Any combination of bus and plane or train will get you there.

Roxboro, North Carolina, ends the trip. Roxboro has only one main bus station, and you can easily reach home from here.

Season

Late fall is the time of year for dry, cold-weather riding. We experienced only two days of rain in the three weeks of riding 950-1,000 total miles. Cold clear mornings and afternoons always kept us at our peak cycling performance. Be sure to pack cool-weather clothing for cycling in the higher altitudes. I'm sure that if the tour were ridden during the summer months it could be completed in less time, due to longer daylight hours.

Accommodations

You can combine hotel/motel accommodations with camping as both facilities are abundant along this route.

Level of Difficulty

I would suggest this particular tour to anyone who enjoys bike-packing any type of terrain. I think that this certain route from Massachusetts to North Carolina could be enjoyed by all different ages, as long as they are physically and mentally prepared. The traffic was always light on the back roads we followed.

MASSACHUSETTS TO NORTH CAROLINA TOUR

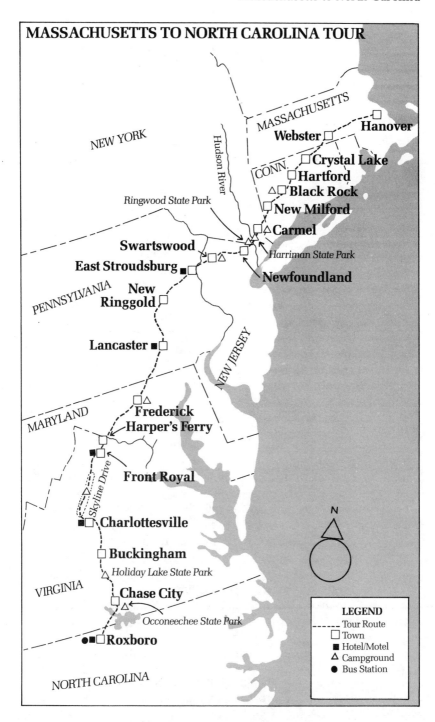

NEW YORK

MASSACHUSETTS

Hudson River

Hanover

Webster

CONN.

Crystal Lake

Hartford

Black Rock

New Milford

Ringwood State Park

Carmel

Swartswood

Harriman State Park

East Stroudsburg

Newfoundland

PENNSYLVANIA

New Ringgold

Lancaster

NEW JERSEY

Frederick

Harper's Ferry

MARYLAND

Front Royal

Skyline Drive

N

Charlottesville

Buckingham

Holiday Lake State Park

VIRGINIA

Chase City

Occoneechee State Park

Roxboro

NORTH CAROLINA

LEGEND
- - - - - Tour Route
☐ Town
■ Hotel/Motel
△ Campground
● Bus Station

References

State road maps of the particular states involved in this tour are the best information sources.

Tour Outline and Points of Interest

Day 1 — Hanover to Hopedale, Massachusetts — 40 miles. Take Route 27 north from Hanover to Brockton, Massachusetts, a 10-mile distance. Follow 27 north to Route 109 south and continue on for 15 miles to Milford, Massachusetts. From there follow 109 south to Hopedale, Massachusetts, for the evening. We camped at a sewerage treatment plant. It is a very easy route to follow from any map. There was a small amount of traffic on this day, so we took all of the scenic back roads. There are plenty of accommodations available in any of the towns encountered for those who would rather stay inside. The terrain is mostly hilly, but never too difficult to pedal with a loaded bike. The roads are in good shape, except for a few frost heaves scattered about. Drinking water can be found in any service station.

Day 2 — Hopedale, Massachusetts, to Lake Champlain, Connecticut — 50 miles. Heading south again you'll be on Route 16 for 30 miles before coming to the Connecticut border. This part of Massachusetts/Connecticut is really tranquil country. You'll pick up Route 197 off of 16 in Webster, Massachusetts. Continue south on Route 197 into Connecticut's beautiful back roads through valley farmlands. We stayed at a scenic campground at Lake Champlain, Connecticut. We were the only people there because of the time of year, which we liked even more. The hills start to increase in elevation now, so get your legs geared-up for some hill climbing. This time of year only gives you until 4:00 or 4:30 P.M. before it's dark, so you will want to break camp around 3:30 at the latest. This is the main reason why you can't do 100+ miles a day. There aren't any hotels or motels in this area of Connecticut, but plenty of woods for camping wherever you look. There are small streams with clean drinking water running off the larger hills on the side of the road. As before, traffic was almost nonexistent.

Day 3 — Lake Champlain to New Britain, Connecticut — 60 miles. Leaving Lake Champlain campground, proceed southwest on Route 197, which is a scenic back road, for about 15 miles of up-and-down bicycling. On this day, the heavy woodlands to the north greatly reduced the wind velocity. Again, drinking water can be obtained from the many clean-running mountain streams along these roads. Route 197 then joins with Route 190 south to Crystal Lake, which is a really unique town, along with the great people who work and reside here. From here, Route 30 south and Route 140 south are confusing to follow, but either one offers exceptional traveling through the wilderness. These routes eventually take you to Hartford, Connecticut, about 25 to 30 miles from Crystal Lake. We went right through the center of Hartford to get to central Connecticut State College in New Britain. Take Interstate 5 until you reach the signs which point the way to the college. Colleges are great places to shower up and relate your experiences to people along the way. We just asked some students if they had a six-foot sleeping space for the night, and we never had any trouble on the whole trip. This area has numerous hotels and motels for those wishing this type of environment, and customer and tourist information is available almost anywhere.

Day 4 — New Britain to Black Rock Lake, Connecticut — 40 miles. Setting out in a westerly direction from the college, pick up Route 72 to Terryville, 20 miles. In Terryville, we ate lunch because we had a late start this day. Proceed on to a beautiful state park known as Black Rock Lake, via Route 6. These are very easy roads to follow. All in all the roads and terrain were a lot easier to travel out of New Britain than the previous three days of hilly riding. Drinking water is available for the asking anywhere along these routes, and at the state park. A few miles north you can cycle around the circumference of Black Rock Lake's large reservoir and dam. Again, the traffic was minimal along these peaceful back roads. Access to food and other conveniences is plentiful along these routes, as well.

Day 5 — Black Rock Lake, Connecticut, to Lake Carmel, New York — 65 miles. Heading south on Route 6, we aimed our sights at Woodbury, Connecticut, 15 miles, where we picked up Route 317 west for Roxbury. Here is where I climbed some of the steepest and quickest increases in elevation throughout the whole trip, so be physically and mentally prepared to do some heavy touring in these parts. Route 317 from Woodbury to Roxbury is close to 10 miles of ups and downs. From Roxbury get onto Route 67 heading to New Milford. Again the elevations reach the 1,000-foot range, as you are now drawing closer to the Appalachian Mountains. We found plenty of places for lunch located in New Milford. Then take Route 37 west to New York. From New Milford to the New York border is about 15 to 20 miles. There are plenty of clean-running streams along the side of the roads traveled here. We saw only about 50 cars on this day. From the border to Carmel, New York, is around 20 miles. Route 164 will run into 301, and then forward to Lake Carmel, where we spent our evening. Carmel is the only town since New Milford with any tourist information or stores, so keep this in mind if you run

27

short before reaching Carmel. This part of New York is really impressive for those who are looking to get away from the hustle and bustle of their larger cities.

Day 6 — Lake Carmel, New York, to Ringwood, New Jersey — 60 miles. Leaving Lake Carmel head in a northwesterly direction on Route 301 to Kent Cliffs, New York. In the center of town is one small general store, so if any supplies are needed, here is a good place to stop. From here stay on Route 301 and cross over the Appalachian Trail about 10 to 15 miles from Carmel. Route 301 south is a bicyclist's dream road. After climbing for about one mile uphill, you then can cruise downhill many miles until you reach Route 9D, where you can cross the Hudson River at the same spot the Appalachian Trail does. Even though this is the dirtiest river to be found along the tour, the scenery is gorgeous. Total mileage from Carmel to the Hudson is 25 miles or so. Once you are across the bridge (no toll for bikes), get on Route 9W south to Stony Point, which is 8 to 10 miles farther. This road follows along the Hudson, and there are two enjoyable bike routes for cyclists only. From Stony Point, Route 210 west will bring you into the beautiful Harriman State Park of New York. This was the ultimate ride for us because the sun was late in setting this day, and it gave us more time to savor the beauty here. Picking up Route 17 south will take you to New Jersey and the incredible Ringwood State Park. Total miles from Stony Point to Ringwood, New Jersey, is 25 miles. There is a church which plays organs, bells, and chimes every hour on the hour at Ringwood, which will lull any cyclist to sleep after a hard day's ride. Drinking water will be found anywhere along these roads.

Day 7 — Ringwood to Swartswood Lake, New Jersey — 50 miles. After a beautiful stay at Ringwood State Park, we continue southwest to Route 513 and West Milford, 10 to 15 miles. This day's ride consists of back roads that are not marked as routes, so follow your compass and ask many people for directions to your destination this night, Swartswood Lake. Route 513 south will bring you to Newfoundland, New Jersey, and here is where you switch to the back roads that follow rolling hills to the town of Newton, New Jersey. It's advisable to do all the shopping needed for that night here, and there is an excellent bike shop located in the middle of town. The person who runs the shop encounters many bikepackers every year, and he'll surely take care of anything you need. Newfoundland to Newton is a distance of 25 miles. From Newton to Lake Swartswood Park is 5 miles. This is a beautiful park nestled in among the pine groves, with cool clean-running water available. The Appalachian Trail is your next-door neighbor on this part of the route, so anyone who enjoys a little backpacking will find this an added endeavor.

Day 8 — Swartswood Lake, New Jersey, to East Stroudsburg, Pennsylvania — 30 miles. Hop onto Route 521 south toward Blairstown, 15 miles. From here, take Route 94 south to the border of Pennsylvania, which is another ten miles. Reaching the Delaware River, cross on Route 611 north which follows the river up to the Delaware Water Gap. This is a fantastic ride along the river, with many overlooks and rest stops to view the natural beauty of Pennsylvania. We decided to stay in a motel this night in East Stroudsburg, Pennsylvania. The uptown motel, $20 a night for two people and super accommodations, felt terrific after being on the road nonstop for eight days. The roads in this area are the cement type with gaps every 25 feet which can ruin your wheels, so extra caution is required when cruising these routes. Dale's Bike Shop in East Stroudsburg is a very reputable dealer, and will take care of your cycling needs. The rolling hills are a real pleasure to cycle along here in Pennsylvania, with numerous meadows to your left and right.

Day 9 — East Stroudsburg to New Ringgold, Pennsylvania — 50 miles. Leaving East Stroudsburg, take Route 209 south to Sciota, Pennsylvania, 5 to 10 miles. Here you pick up a back road that is parallel with the Appalachian Trail for about 40 miles. This is superb riding terrain for those who like rolling hills with the mountains always in view. From Sciota to Palmerton, Pennsylvania, is around 20 miles. There are plenty of convenience shops and information on the land and roads in Palmerton. A big zinc smelter dominates Palmerton, but once through this and onto Route 895, you are back into nature. Palmerton to New Ringgold, Pennsylvania, is also 20 miles. Here we stayed at a Boy Scout reservation camp for two days. The only way to find this place is to ask at the general store in New Ringgold, and the owner will give you directions. He was really helpful and said that he sees only a handful of bikepackers every year, so he does all he can for you. On arriving, there were Scouts already there, and they cooked us some dinner that night. In the morning it was raining, so we decided to take that well-wanted rest day. To show our appreciation to the Scouts, we built a sweat, or homemade sauna, for them. We cut saplings about 15 feet long and stuck each end into the ground to create a dome shape. We then draped it with a plastic drop cloth and sealed it with dirt along the bottom. Then we threw tents, sleeping bags, and blankets over this to act as an insulator for the heat. We heated about 10 rocks in a large fire for a few hours and brought them inside the sweat with a couple gallons of water and there you have it; best way to loosen those tight quadriceps, too.

Day 10 — New Ringgold to Lancaster, Pennsylvania — 55 miles. Pick up Route 895 south once again and cross over the Appalachian Trail on your way to Womelsdorf, Pennsylvania, 30 miles. After crossing the trail you'll be on Route 419 south. Be ready for some serious uphill climbing for a few miles. Continue on 419 south until 501 south toward Lancaster, Pennsylvania. The distance from Womelsdorf to Lancaster is around 25 miles. This is Amish country, which is quite beautiful. The lands are all patchworks of different colors and contours, with the people dressed in their styles of clothing and riding only horse and buggies. It really makes you appreciate your bicycle touring 100 percent. The last 30 miles are more like rolling plains than hills, so you can cover a lot of miles with the wind at your back. We spent the night at Franklin and Marshall College after meeting a student who lived in a fraternity house there. Lancaster is a large community, so again anything needed for the bikepacker will be here. We encountered more traffic here in Lancaster than anywhere else.

Day 11 — Lancaster, Pennsylvania, to Westminster, Maryland — 50 miles. We ended up staying for two nights at Franklin and Marshall College due to rain. Head west on Route 462 from the college to the Susquehanna River, about 10 miles. From Columbia, Pennsylvania, pick up Route 214 south, a remote back road to Loganville, Pennsylvania, where it joins with 216 south toward Maryland, around 30 miles to the border. From here, we set our sights on Western Maryland College for another night. At the border, Route 216 south changes into Route 86 south for 5 to 10 miles. When reaching Manchester, Maryland, hop onto Route 27 south, which is a beautiful road with very little traffic, and this will bring you right to the college via road signs. Maryland's roads are kept in top shape so they are a joy to cycle. About ½ mile from the college is a campground open only in the summer, and there are a few hotels/motels in this area. The terrain traveled is quite hilly from Lancaster, Pennsylvania, to Westminster, Maryland. Unfortunately, drinking water was to be found only in a gas station's tap or other public places.

Day 12 — Westminster, Maryland, to Harper's Ferry, Virginia — 45 miles. Proceed south on Route 31 from Westminster, Maryland, for 25 miles to the city of Frederick. From Frederick take Route 180 south for 20 miles to Harper's Ferry. This section of the ride is very intense due to the strong head winds. It took us three hours to go the distance. We camped outside of a youth hostel at Harper's Ferry for free. There is also a state park located in Harper's Ferry. Food, drinking water, and other necessities are plentiful in this area. Harper's Ferry is quite a tourist attraction, and it is located on three different states' borders (West Virginia, Virginia, and Mary-

land). The terrain is still hilly but not mountainous yet. Your guide-
line, the Appalachian Trail, crosses your path here in Harper's Ferry
once again.

Day 13 — *Harper's Ferry to Front Royal, Virginia* — *55 miles.*
Use Route 340 south, which is heavily traveled by motor vehicles.
The roads are in good shape, except for an occasional frost heave,
and the terrain is rolling hills heading to the Shenandoah Mountains.
There are plenty of towns on this road so all supplies can be found
easily on the way. Front Royal, Virginia, is a very large place and
motels/hotels are everywhere. As for campgrounds, there is a KOA
campground located near the entrance of Skyline Drive.

Day 14 — *Front Royal to Big Meadows Campground,
Virginia* — *51 miles.* With an excellent breakfast tucked away, head
on to the mountains of Shenandoah Valley. There is an entrance fee
for cyclists during the warmer months. The park is 105.4 miles of
incredible overlooks, mountains, wildlife, and camping areas. You
should have your legs prepared for some heavy-duty climbing. Roads
are in excellent condition, and traffic minimal except in summer.
There are mile markers along the side of the road for those interested.
Information and supplies are available just about anywhere in the
park. The pamphlet you get before entering explains everything
needed to know for sights, adventures, and backpacking. On this day
we counted 21 white-tailed deer grazing off on the sides of the road.
Also, hawks are everywhere and the park seems to come alive with
animals.

Day 15 — *Big Meadows Campground to Charlottesville, Virginia* — *55 miles.* This day we encountered heavy winds, in our
favor though, blowing from the northeast. We covered the last 53
miles of Skyline Drive very quickly and the drive doesn't start to
decline until the very last mile. We came out of Skyline Drive and
decided that we wouldn't stay in the mountains any longer. We were
going to travel the Blue Ridge Parkway, but this time of year made
it difficult. We came across snow on Skyline Drive, but it was so
windy that it was blown off the road. We headed east on Route 240
for the University of Virginia in Charlottesville, which was about 20
miles from Waynesboro, Virginia. We met some friendly people here
who put us up for the night. Again, the supplies needed were always
available after the Skyline Drive.

Day 16 — *Charlottesville to Holiday Lake State Park, Virginia* — *60 miles.* Heading out on Route 250 east for 5 miles brings
you to Route 20 south, a very remote, rarely traveled back road.
Follow this route for about 30 miles to Buckingham, Virginia. From
here, take Route 640 south to Holiday Lake State Park, 20 miles.
These roads are heavily graveled in parts and feel like they are eating

your tires. You'll come to a Trading Post (Anderson's) on this road, and if you need anything, this is the place to get it. A wonderful woman lives here and sells groceries. These roads are very confusing so ask this lady and she'll direct you the right way. Appomattox Historic Park is also in this area for camping. And there are a few dirt roads to cycle to get to Holiday Lake State Park, so be ready to do some slow riding. I suggest getting your drinking water in Buckingham for the ride to the park. The park has all necessary facilities, too.

Day 17 — Holiday Lake State Park to Occoneechee State Park, Virginia — 65 miles. When leaving Holiday Lake State Park, you should ask the ranger for the easiest directions to get to Route 47 south. These roads are confusing, and I don't know of any map that shows all of the back roads here. When reaching Route 47 south, follow it for a good 40 miles until you reach Chase City, Virginia. The terrain is easily covered here for it is rolling hills and the roads are the best for high-speed touring. At Chase City, we picked up Route 49 south to Occoneechee State Park, Virginia, 15 miles. There are plenty of food stores and places to get drinking water along the way. Occoneechee State Park is a really nice spot to camp, but you can cross the bridge to Clarksville, Virginia, and find many hotels/motels for your convenience.

Day 18 — Occoneechee State Park, Virginia, to Roxboro, North Carolina — 30 miles. Follow Route 49 south again to the border of North Carolina, 15 miles, and onto Roxboro, North Carolina, another 15 miles. The roads are very hilly along this route. There is one main bus station in Roxboro which can take you anywhere you'd like.

Notes

Touring Bucks County, Pennsylvania

Location

Beautiful upper Bucks County rewards all bikers with its lovely scenic hills and numerous points of interest. On this 44-mile tour you will roll by lakes, mountains, rivers, waterfalls, wildlife, farms, and historical sites. The nearest town to this tour is Quakertown, Pennsylvania, which is accessible by both train and bus. If arriving by car, exit the Pennsylvania Turnpike at exit 32. Proceed east for nine miles on Route 663 which turns into Route 313. Five miles beyond town, turn left onto Three Mile Run Road. One mile on the left is a boat ramp parking lot where you can leave your car parked for the trip.

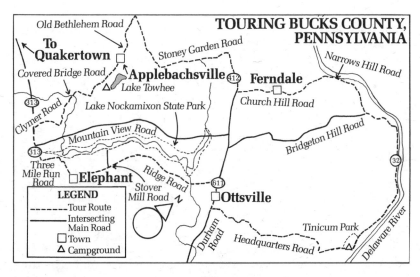

33

Season

Touring Bucks County in the springtime allows you to witness the awakening of the surroundings, but be careful of potholes, remnants of the preceding winter. Summers may be too hot for some (temperatures in the mid to high 80s), but this makes the various lakes, waterfalls, and rivers that much more refreshing. Perhaps fall is the loveliest season of all to tour this area. The air is crisp and clean, and the brilliant foliage is indescribable. Just beware of slippery leaves.

Accommodations

This is a 44-mile tour, so depending on your cycling ability, it may be taken as a one-day trip or a leisurely weekend ride. A good place to stop overnight would be Tinicum Park where camping is available. Lake Towhee also offers camping facilities.

Level of Difficulty

I cannot suggest this course to persons intimidated by hills, curves, bumps, or cars. But on the other hand, if this is the case, riding this route may provide you with the courage, confidence and joy promoted by bicycle touring.

References

Information and maps are available from Lake Nockamixon State Park, Dept. of Environmental Resources, R.D. 3, Box 125A, Quakertown, PA 18951; Bucks County Dept. of Parks and Recreation, Core Creek Park, Box 358, R.D. 1, Langhorne, PA 19047; Doylestown Court House, Doylestown, PA 18901.

Tour Outline and Points of Interest

Three Mile Run Road boat landing, in Lake Nockamixon State Park, is a great starting point for a one-day ride. Turn left out of the parking lot to the stop sign in front of the Region Park Office. Turn right past Lake House Inn, go through the stop sign. Wind around the long S turn and on up to Elephant Hotel. Founded in 1748, this establishment was once under British rule. Turn left on Ridge Road, you will soon roll by Upper Bucks Technical School. Take the next left onto Stover Mill Road. Stop by at the first farm on your left and take a look at two peacocks in their private pen. Return back to Ridge Road and continue for 1½ miles for an impressive view of Keller's Church. This huge stone church was founded in 1741 and is proudly situated before a background of Lake Nockamixon and Mt. Haycock. Well, now there's only 2½ miles between you and a dam. One mile up is brand new road surface. The slope is mild and the view spectacular. From the top it is 1½ miles down to the dam. You may zip right by unless you look or listen for it. Soon after the dam, you head uphill to Route 611. Here Ridge Road ends on Route 611 by the Landmark Inn. It's a great place for a beer, but it's probably too early. Directly across the parking lot is Durham Road. This road begins running south, parallel with and then disappearing left of Route 611. Take this south down a quick 1½ miles past one intersection to your first left past Ottsville Inn. Turn left. You are now on Headquarters Road which has its rough spots. Potholes must be watched for during the spring. Six miles of winding uphill and turning down over two fair-sized hills and along two sparkling creeks will get you to the Delaware River. These hills aren't safe for racing, so plan to take it easy. There are sharp curves in both, and a stop sign at the bottom of the last hill.

Turn right at the stop sign to Delaware Canal, a few yards away. Go left ¼ mile up canal to Tinicum Park. This is a super spot to rest, camp, picnic, or play games in the small woods and large meadows.

When leaving, make a left out of Tinicum onto River Road (Route 32 north). This road has a smooth surface, but also many curves with small shoulders. Traffic is light, except on weekend afternoons. These hazards seem minor once you start rolling alongside the last major free-flowing river in the United States (no major dams). It never fails to inspire and amaze me with the path it has cut. In six miles the second bridge you will pass is Milford Bridge. A tenth mile past is Bridgeton Hill Road. Make a left and crank up the monster mountain of the tour. You might wish to stop for food at the store by the canal.

When you've conquered this climb, a break is deserved at Ringing Rocks Park. Turn right on Ringing Rocks Road (second right). Here you may bang a tune on rocks in Boulder Field. These rocks really do ring. And you can cool off by the waterfalls.

From Ringing Rocks, continue to the end of this road. Turn left up Narrows Hill Road. This takes you up 1½ miles to an excellent profile view of Mt. Haycock, largest mountain in Bucks County. Then it's down a little over ½ mile to the only stoplight on the tour. Make a left and a quick right around Ferndale Inn. This is now Church Hill Road which rolls up and down 2½ miles to Palisades High School on Route 412. Turn right on Route 412 north for 1½ miles to Stoney Point Store and the Walking Purchase marker.

From the marker, return to the road you have passed ¹/₁₀ mile back and make a right onto Stoney Garden Road. This road offers some great curves which are evenly banked, but beware of the one-lane bridge about a mile from Route 412. You will come to a fork, but either way takes you to Old Bethlehem Road. Turn left on Old Bethlehem Road through Applebachsville to Lake Towhee on the left.

Lake Towhee offers camping, hiking trail, boat rental, and is a sanctuary for Canada geese. Downhill from Towhee is Parkway Drive Inn, a fine place for munchies and miniature golfing. Turn right here on Thatcher Road to the second left at the snowmobile dealer. Then cycle a short distance to Sheard's Mill Covered Bridge built in 1873.

At the end of the road (Covered Bridge Road), turn left onto Union Road and it's a short ride to Weisel Park and Youth Hostel. Clymer Road is directly across from the park on your right. Cycling up the road you will discover a magnificent garden (complete with chapel and pyramids), a publishing company, a health clinic, and a health food store. After an uphill mile to the stop sign, it's a mile downhill to Mountain View Road and Route 313.

You should now be ready to use the skills this tour encourages. It's left on Route 313 east, straight down ½ mile and up $3/10$ mile to Three Mile Run Road. Traffic is heavy so the wary cyclist may want to walk. Turning left on Three Mile Run Road leaves you 1 mile from the starting point.

Notes

Touring in the
Greater Miami Area

Location

For the cyclist coming into Miami to begin a tour in Florida, there are many directions to go in and many things to see. This tour concentrates primarily on riding through the Everglades National Park, the third largest park in our National Parks system. Directions are also given for tours radiating in other directions from the Miami area.

At the present time Amtrak serves Miami, but use caution as the station is located in a very tough section of the city. Both Greyhound and Trailways have a bus station downtown.

Season

From May to September it is often hot and the humidity is high. Along with the summer heat are the frequent rains, perfect for mosquito breeding. If touring at this time of year, bring along the raingear, sunscreen, and bug repellent. If you are camping out, a tent with mosquito netting is a must. October to February is the most pleasant time of year to cycle in Florida. Count on shifting winds.

Accommodations

North Miami has a KOA campground at U.S. 1 and N.W. 140 Street, and Dade County has one, Thompson Park, just off U.S. 27. There are a multitude of motels around the airport and on U.S. 1 both north and south. However, after leaving the airport area and on the south route, there are none until Homestead. If riding west, you had better count on camping at least one night in the Everglades. North on U.S. 27 there are no motels until Belle Glade. Food is available everywhere along all routes.

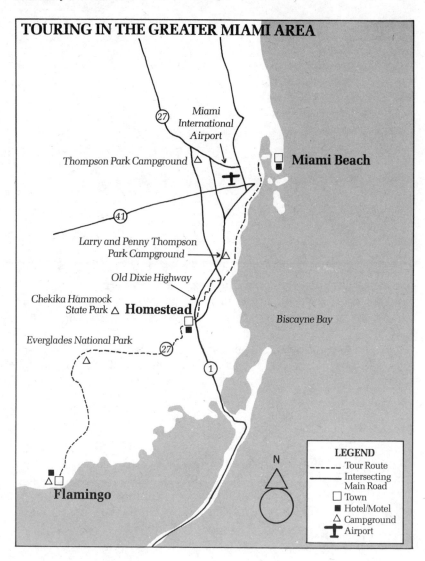

TOURING IN THE GREATER MIAMI AREA

Miami International Airport

Thompson Park Campground

Miami Beach

27

41

Larry and Penny Thompson Park Campground

Old Dixie Highway

Chekika Hammock State Park **Homestead**

Everglades National Park

Biscayne Bay

27

1

Flamingo

LEGEND
- - - - Tour Route
——— Intersecting Main Road
□ Town
■ Hotel/Motel
△ Campground
✈ Airport

N

Level of Difficulty

There is just one word to describe Southern Florida—flat. Even the beginner bicycle tourist will find this area to be conducive to leisurely cycling.

38

References

For Florida state maps write to the Department of Commerce, Division of Tourism, 107 W. Gaines St., Tallahassee, FL 32304. For information and maps of the Everglades contact the Superintendent, Everglades National Park, Box 279, Homestead, FL 33030.

Tour Outline and Points of Interest

From Miami International Airport to points south and west: From the unloading area ride east to the first exit onto Perimeter Road (becomes Weatherford Road or N.W. 12 Street). Circle around the FAA building by making a short dog leg. Ride west along the airport fence past Milam Dairy Road (N.W. 72 Avenue) to Galloway Road (S.W. 87 Avenue, 5 miles). Turn left onto Galloway Road and go south to Tamiami Trail (U.S. 41, 1.3 miles). This highway will take you to the west coast (Naples, Tampa).

To reach Thompson Park Campground (county-run with hot/cold showers) ride west on Tamiami Trail (U.S. 41) to Krome Avenue (U.S. 27 or S.W. 177 Avenue, 9 miles). Turn right on Krome Avenue and go north to the park (9 miles). From Thompson Park you can reach points in north and central Florida. From Thompson Park north to Belle Glade (50 miles), U.S. 27 is a narrow and dangerous two-lane road. At this date it is under construction for a four-lane. I do not recommend cycling this stretch until construction is completed.

For points south (Homestead, Everglades National Park, Key West) continue south on Galloway Road to Miller Drive (S.W. 56 Street, 4.3 miles). Turn right and go west on Miller Drive to S.W. 102 Avenue (1.5 miles). Turn left and go south on S.W. 102 Avenue to Sunset Drive (S.W. 72 Street, 1 mile). Turn right and go west on Sunset Drive to S.W. 137 Avenue (3.5 miles). Turn left and go south on S.W. 137 Avenue past Tamiami Airport to S.W. 160 Street (just before the federal prison, 5 miles).

To reach Larry and Penny Thompson Park Campground continue south on S.W. 137 Avenue. Make a short dog leg and you are there.

To continue to points south turn right off S.W. 137 Avenue onto S.W. 160 Street and ride west to S.W. 147 Avenue (1 mile). Turn left and go south on S.W. 147 Avenue (Naranja Road). To reach Chekika Hammock State Park campground turn right off Naranja Road onto Quail Roost Drive (S.W. 200 Street, 2.5 miles). Ride west to Redland Road (S.W. 187 Avenue, 4 miles). Turn right and go north on Redland Road to Grossman Farm Road (0.5 mile). Turn left and go west on Grossman Farm Road to the park (6 miles). To reach the KOA turn right onto Quail Roost Drive from Naranja Road and ride west to Farm Life Road (School Road or S.W. 162 Avenue, 1.5 miles). Turn left and go south on Farm Life Road and ride the short distance to the KOA. To reach Homestead continue south on Naranja Road until it meets Old Dixie Highway near S.W. 264 Street (6.5 miles). Old Dixie Highway runs directly into Homestead (2.5 miles).

To reach Key West, exit off Old Dixie Highway onto U.S. 1 (they run parallel). From here U.S. 1 is a narrow, crowded, dangerous highway. It is also the only route.

To reach Everglades National Park turn right off Old Dixie Highway onto Avocado Drive (S.W. 296 Street). Cycle west to Loveland Road (S.W. 217 Avenue, five miles). Turn left and go south to U.S. 27 (six miles). At U.S. 27 turn right and go west to the park entrance (two miles).

Once past the visitor's entrance, cycle to the Royal Palm Area. Here the Anhingua Trail, named after the bird of the same name, has the best watering hole or slough for viewing wildlife in the park. There are cold drinks, restrooms, exhibit areas, and guided walks from Royal Palm. Gumbo Limbo Trail goes through a tropical hardwood forest.

Four miles into the park is the Long Pine Key Area and a campground. This is the last water source until West Lake, 26 miles distant. In another 2.5 miles you'll find Pineland Trail, a trail through a pinewood community. At mile 12.5 is Pa-hay-okee, or river of grass, which has a boardwalk and tower to give you a real appreciation of the park.

Mahogany Hammock, at mile 19.5, contains the oldest mahogany tree in existence. The boardwalk here is several miles from the main road. If you'd like to have a picnic, travel onward to Paurotis Pond with limited facilities and a view of rare palms.

The fresh water from Lake Okeechobee gives way to the salt water from Florida Bay at West Lake, at mile 30.5. Stiltlike mangrove swamps, characteristic of salt water, are everywhere.

Your final destination is Flamingo with its many services. There are campgrounds for tents, charcoal burners, picnic tables, cold water showers, a small general store, a restaurant, a motel, a visitor center, exhibits, and naturalist programs. All hiking and canoe trails start from here.

From Miami International Airport to points north: To reach the east coast there are many routes from the airport to U.S. 1 or A1A. The easiest route has the heaviest traffic and passes through some of the rougher areas of the city. Exit the airport area by heading north on LeJune Road (N.W. 8 Avenue or N.W. 42 Avenue) to N.W. 36

Street and turn right (1 mile). Ride east to U.S. 1 (Biscayne Boulevard, 4.5 miles). From N.W. 36 Street and Biscayne Boulevard the route north is your option.

To reach Central Florida via U.S. 27, follow the directions to Thompson Park given earlier or exit the airport area and proceed north on LeJune Road (N.W. 8 Avenue or N.W. 42 Avenue). Follow the signs for U.S. 27 (Okeechobee Road, one mile). Expect plenty of traffic to the city limits (about five miles), and from there to Belle Glade. U.S. 27 is 95 percent two-lane with loads of heavy truck traffic. At this date U.S. 27 is under construction to four-lane.

Through Miami north to south: Entering Dade County on U.S. 1, ride south to N.W. 36 Street. Follow the reverse directions given earlier to the airport and points south.

Or you can enter Dade County on U.S. 1 and take this highway through Miami to the start of the present marked north-south bike route. Pick up the marked bike route ¼ mile south of U.S. 1 and Rickenbacker Causeway, on South Bayshore Drive. South Bayshore Drive forks off from U.S. 1 and follows the bay's edge. This marked route will take you to Homestead.

Or enter Dade County via A1A (Miami Beach). From the beach cross the bay on General Douglas MacArthur Causeway and connect up with U.S. 1 (Biscayne Boulevard).

Notes

Duneland:
A Western Michigan Ride

Location

The word Michigan is derived from the Algonquian Indians and means land surrounded by great waters, which makes it a beautiful area for bicycle touring. This tour begins and ends in Ludington and heads north to the tip of the Leelanau Peninsula and back south again. It is a total of approximately 300 miles filled with views of lakes, dunes, islands, peninsulas, and well-paved roads for biking.

Ludington is accessible only by car, bus, or ferry (from Wisconsin). Commercial flights are available to Manistee and Traverse City.

Season

Summer is the most enjoyable time of year to take this tour. Temperatures range between 80° and 85°F. Be sure to take along raingear and anticipate heavy winds (northwest) along the lakeshore.

Accommodations

Accommodations never seem to be a problem on this route. There are numerous campgrounds, motels, cabins, and restaurants throughout the entire tour. This is, after all, a heavy tourist land.

Level of Difficulty

This is a fantastic one-week tour for any novice cyclist. The terrain is mostly moderate rolling hills, with the exception of a few very high and steep dunes. The roads are of high quality with moderate traffic.

References

Excellent county maps with tour descriptions entitled "Biking

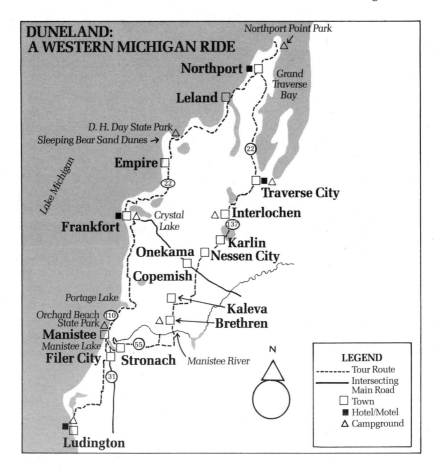

DUNELAND:
A WESTERN MICHIGAN RIDE

Northport Point Park

Northport ■□
Grand
Traverse
Bay

Leland □

D. H. Day State Park
Sleeping Bear Sand Dunes →

Empire □

Lake Michigan

22

□■△
Traverse City

△□Interlochen

137

Frankfort
■□△ Crystal
Lake

□Karlin
Onekama □Nessen City

Copemish

Portage Lake

Orchard Beach □□
State Park △

Manistee □
Manistee Lake
Filer City □ Stronach   *Manistee River*

Kaleva
Brethren

110

△□

55

31

N

LEGEND
------- Tour Route
——— Intersecting
Main Road
□ Town
■ Hotel/Motel
△ Campground

■□
Ludington

Western Michigan" are available from the Western Michigan Tourist Association, 136 E. Fulton St., Grand Rapids, MI 49503. You can obtain a map of Leelanau County with a calendar of events from the Leelanau County Chamber of Commerce, Rt. 2, Box 466, Suttons Bay, MI 49682. An adequate Michigan state map is also useful for this particular tour.

Tour Outline and Points of Interest

Day 1 — Ludington to Orchard Beach State Park — 35 miles. Follow back roads and avoid the heavy traffic on U.S. 31. Leaving Ludington, you're parallel to U.S. 31 into Manistee. This takes you past the Lake Michigan campground of Manistee National Forest

43

which offers many miles of dunes and woods for hiking and camping. Camp at Orchard Beach State Park.

Day 2 — Orchard Beach State Park to Frankfort — 30 miles. The second day may be the most strenuous, although you'll only cover 30 miles. Continue from Orchard Beach State Park on 110 to Portage Lake where the road merges with 22 and follow north. At Onekama on Portage Lake there is a very inviting picnic park with a swimming beach. The western shore is characterized by dunes and river bottom lands and you'll soon discover that every town is on a river, so that the approach is a pleasant ride downhill but the departure can be difficult. These very high and steep hills are a result of the wave and wind action during the existence of the glacial Lake Nippising, which covered the area of the present Lake Michigan and several miles inland. The higher water level created giant dunes that are now partially stabilized by vegetation and can be quite a distance from the actual beach. The highest dune is north of Arcadia and the view at the top is magnificent. The last really high dune is north of Herring Lakes.

Frankfort is a nice town with several restaurants, a deli, a movie theater, art studios, motels, a car ferry port, natural mineral springs at the marina, and a pier with a lighthouse. Camping is available at the Betsie River Camp (two miles southeast of town).

Day 3 — Frankfort to D. H. Day State Park — 35 miles. The next day continue on 22, winding your way among the lakes toward Sleeping Bear Sand Dunes. You'll pass by Benzie State Park. North of there lies Crystal Lake, surrounded by two high, tree-covered glacial moraines running east and west. The ride to Empire is easy, gliding through pine forests and flat farmland. The rest of the ride is a little more hilly but much easier than the previous day's riding.

The Sleeping Bear Sand Dunes, the largest, moving dunes in the world, are not to be passed by. They are the best example of the postglacial inland dunes and are perched on coastal dunes 450 feet above Lake Michigan. The climb to the top, with the resulting view of miles of sand stretching to the big lake, and the run down are nearly unbelievable. The sand dune's name is from an Indian legend about a mother bear and her two cubs who attempted to swim from Wisconsin to Michigan. The mother bear reached the shore and turned to wait for her cubs, who succumbed to the waves. In their place rose two islands and the sleeping mother bear eventually turned into a monument of sand.

You can camp at D. H. Day State Park, located several miles northeast of the Dunes. This is a large park with a beautiful swimming beach, pit toilets, and hand-pumped water. It is also a haven for maurading raccoons, so hang all of your food out of their reach as they will chew through panniers, tents, and even coolers to get at your goodies.

Day 4 — D. H. Day State Park to Northport Point Park — 40 miles. The fourth day begins a tour through the Leelanau Peninsula. The countryside has rolling farmlands of cherry trees, strawberries, and grapes for local wineries. Boat rides are available in Leland for tours of lighthouses and shipwrecks or for transportation to North Manitou Island for hiking.

Pushing onward, you'll cross the peninsula to the town of Northport, which has a tremendous view of Grand Traverse Bay. This town has quite a few restaurants, gift shops, and motels. If you ride ten more miles you'll find campsites at Northport Point Park. This park is small, having only 20 primitive campsites, and is situated on a rocky beach complete with a lighthouse.

Day 5 — Northport Point Park to Traverse City — 35 miles. The eastern shore of the Leelanau Peninsula is particularly beautiful as it is full of small peninsulas and islands. Suttons Bay offers restaurants, a swimming beach, a laundromat, a natural food store, and inexpensive cabins right on the bay. Thirty-five miles south of Northport is Traverse City, the largest city on the tour. Here there are many hotels, motels, restaurants, a state park with camping, a zoo, a large marina, and several bicycle shops.

Day 6 — Traverse City to Manistee National Forest — 60 miles. Depart from Traverse City via back roads. Pass through Long Lake and Interlochen. There is a large state park here between the two lakes, and plenty to do if you enjoy the cultural arts.

From Interlochen follow 137 through Karlin, Nessen City, and Copemish; eventually turning west to Kaleva. Turn south to the town of Brethren. Continue south out of Brethren and cross the Manistee River Valley, turn westward on M55 for several miles, and then travel on to Manistee National Forest. The national forest is full of small campgrounds which are semi-private without fees, and are always located on a lake or river surrounded by miles of woods.

Day 7 — Manistee National Forest to Ludington — 45 miles. Take M55 westward, skirt around Manistee Lake via Stronach and Filer City, cross 31 and refollow the original route back to Ludington, which results in a 45-mile day.

As for accommodations in Ludington, just about anything can be had for the traveler. There is a large state park north of town and two small campgrounds south of the bay. The town itself is loaded with motels, restaurants, bars, laundromats, a movie theater, museum, and a good ice cream store.

This part of Michigan is full of beautiful areas and attractions to interest almost anyone.

Notes

Big Texas Tour

Location

Nestled in the undeveloped mountains of West Texas is the small ranching community of Fort Davis, and there begins and ends one of the best short tours in Texas. Aside from its beauty, this area is of both historic and scientific importance. Fort Davis National Historic Site houses the remains of a major frontier army post. Twelve miles northwest of Fort Davis lies McDonald Observatory operated by the Astronomy Department of the University of Texas at Austin. Because of the size and relative isolation of Fort Davis, there is no public transportation to the town.

Season

The Davis Mountains are a semi-arid desert environment. As such, the weather is generally cooperative most of the year. The rainy season is usually August to October, and winters can be bitter cold, but even during these periods perfect cycling days occur. The optimum times to visit the Davis Mountains are mid-spring through summer, and mid-to-late fall. The arid nature of this country means that water is not generally available. We have solved the problem by driving the route and stashing water at several points, or by having someone meet us at one of the several roadside parks on the route.

Accommodations

Davis Mountains State Park, which is three miles from Fort Davis, offers the tourist the best accommodations. Indian Lodge offers food and room, and there are plenty of camping sites for those who prefer sleeping outside. Fort Davis has a hotel and several small motels, and all are well maintained.

Level of Difficulty

The Scenic Loop covers over 75 miles of well-maintained state highways. It is the highest road east of the Rockies, at least 5,000 feet in elevation. The terrain varies from flat to rolling hills. There are three steep climbs along the route. Traffic is minimal. Since this is ranching country, there are periodic cattleguards, but we have found them to be no problem.

References

Write to the following addresses for maps and information on touring in this area: Fort Davis Chamber of Commerce, Fort Davis, TX 79734; Davis Mountains State Park, Fort Davis, TX 79734; Fort Davis National Historic Site, Box 1456, Fort Davis, TX 79734; Visitor Center, The University of Texas, McDonald Observatory, Fort Davis, TX 79734; Mr. John Robert Prude, Prude Ranch Camp, Fort Davis, TX 79734.

Tour Outline and Points of Interest

This tour starts by following State Highway 17 two miles to the junction with State 166. From there the road turns west for 23 miles of flat to rolling hills. In this section the rider first passes the Glasscock Vineyard; the Point of Rocks, a roadside park; the Bloy's Camp-meeting grounds, an interdenominational religious meeting held by area families for a week in August; and lastly Barrel Spring, location of a stage station on the Overland Trail.

Five miles past Barrel Spring, State 166 turns north at a junction with Ranch Road 505. Soon after this there begins a steady but gentle climb that culminates in the first of three severe ascents on this ride. This first climb is to the top of H O Canyon, the summit of which is the halfway point of the Loop. The climb into H O is the longest and steepest, but on the other side there are several miles of downhill and flat riding past Sawtooth Mountain. At the end of this stretch is the junction with State Highway 118, and the rider will take this road southeast for the last third of the ride.

This junction also begins the second major climb to the top of Nunn Hill. Here begins several miles of curving hills that eventually end at the approach to McDonald Observatory. About halfway along this stretch is Madera Canyon, a beautiful roadside park. The climb out of Madera Canyon up Fisher Hill is the third and last major climb.

Two miles short of McDonald Observatory, the road branches with State 118 going down the mountain to Fort Davis, and a spur

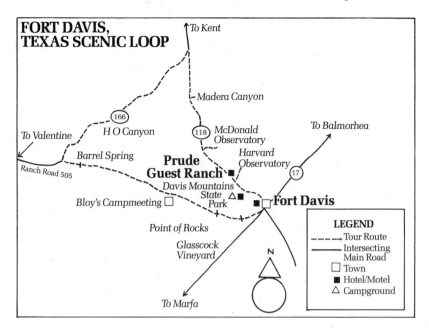

leading up to the observatory proper. This spur is two miles of 17 percent grade that ends at a parking lot. It is a difficult side trip, but the view at the top is worth the effort.

The last 12 miles from the observatory are mostly downhill, with the genuine thrill being the fast descent down Mount Locke. Here the road is wide and the curves gentle. In the last few miles before town the road passes Prude Ranch Camp, the road to the Harvard Radio Observatory, and the entrance to Davis Mountains State Park. The park has a short scenic overlook drive that makes another interesting side trip, or a ride for another day.

The scenery for the whole Loop is beautiful, traffic is minimal since it is off the beaten path, and the roads are well maintained and in excellent condition.

For the last two years there has been an organized ride of the Scenic Loop. Held the first weekend in October and sponsored by the Lubbock Bike Club, the ride attracted almost 70 riders last year. Called the Davis Mountains Bike Fest and Mountain Climb, this ride is hosted by John Robert Prude who operates a summer camp and guest ranch. Prude Ranch Camp is the headquarters for the Bike Fest, and it provides, at a nominal fee, food and lodging for the weekend. On Saturday there is the 75-mile Loop ride with lunch at the halfway point. On Sunday is the mountain climb from the base of Mount Locke to the McDonald Observatory. At an elevation of over 6,000 feet, this is a real test of endurance.

Notes

On the Texas Rio Grande

Location

Big Bend National Park is definitely one of our lesser known national parks. The most probable reason may be because you have to cross the rest of Texas to get to it. Located in the farthest western curve bordering Mexico, it is hard to get to, isolated without public transportation in or out.

The diversity within the 1,100 square miles of park truly offers a lot for those taking enough time to explore the Chisos mountains, surrounding desert, the magnificent canyons and to take an occasional dip in the famous Rio Grande.

This tour started and ended in Marfa, Texas, on U.S. 90. There is an airport in El Paso, 353 miles to the park via Interstate 10, U.S. 90, U.S. 67, and Texas Ranch Road 170. From Del Rio, it is 160 miles via U.S. 90 to Marathon and U.S. 385 to the park headquarters. Amtrak passes along U.S. 90 and stops at Sanderson 125 miles from park headquarters via U.S. 90 and U.S. 385. If you are driving, car storage is available in Presidio. From there it's 98 miles along the Camino del Rio (Texas Ranch Road 170) to the western entrance to the park. It is possible to catch a ride with the mail truck during the week between Alpine and park headquarters.

Season

Big Bend is open all year. Cool weather can be found in the mountains during summer. During winter months the days can be quite pleasant and warm but nights are very cold. The last week of March we experienced quite hot 85° to 100° F. temperatures during the day and quite pleasant evenings. Temperatures vary according to where you are in the park; for example, Boquillas Canyon elevation is 2,113 feet while the Basin is at 5,400 feet.

Accommodations

We camped throughout the park, but there are some motels along the route if you prefer.

Level of Difficulty

Riding along the Rio Grande outside and inside the park is scenic, challenging, and with very little traffic. Much of the river is bordered by sheer rock walls belonging to Mexico. Depending on how much time you have, riding Camino del Rio into the park is worthwhile even if there is a 17 percent grade to conquer. The river road was not especially hilly the direction we went, but you need at least two full days to have time to explore side roads to the river. Going before March would make it more pleasant (not so hot). Carry plenty of water.

References

Write to the Superintendent, Big Bend National Park, TX 79834 for free park brochures and park accommodations list. Available at Panther Junction Park Headquarters are: topographic map of Terlingua-Chisos Mountains; "Guide to the Backcountry Roads and River"; "Road Guide to Big Bend"; and "The Big Bend—A History of the Last Texas Frontier" by Ronnie C. Tyler.

Tour Outline and Points of Interest

Day 1 — Marfa to Presidio on U.S. 67 — 61 miles. You travel through gentle rolling hills for the first 20 miles with some occasional climbing. You'll pass through Shafter, virtually a ghost town, but you can get water there. There is a 1-mile hill out of Shafter, then 19 miles of basic downhill. Presidio is at the junction of 67 and 170. You'll find good stores. Ask about camping in the Lions City Park.

Day 2 — Presidio to Contrabando Creek via 170 — 45 miles. Be prepared as there is no water until Redford, and there only a store and station. The hills are short and steep to "Big Hill" also called Penacho Point. The grade here is 17 percent, the steepest in Texas, but it is only ½ mile long. There is a rest area and shade at the bottom of the hill, but no water. Contrabando Creek offers some very nice camping spots along the river.

Day 3 — Contrabando Creek to Santa Elena Canyon — 41 miles. It's a short 5 miles to Lajitas (flat rocks) where there is a restaurant and store. Continuing on to Terlingua, a ghost town from mercury mining days, there is very low traffic. Study Butte houses a campground. From here it's 2 miles to the park entrance and 1 mile into

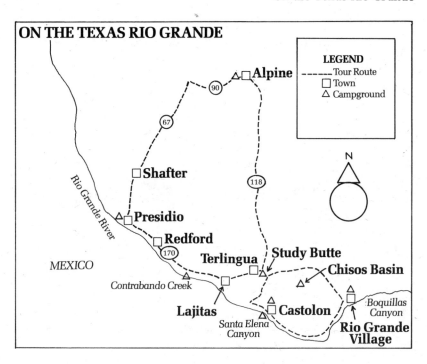

ON THE TEXAS RIO GRANDE

LEGEND
- - - Tour Route
☐ Town
△ Campground

N

Alpine
90
67
Shafter
Rio Grande River
Presidio
Redford
170
Terlingua
Study Butte
Chisos Basin
118
MEXICO
Contrabando Creek
Lajitas
Santa Elena Canyon
Castolon
Boquillas Canyon
Rio Grande Village

the park to Maverick. The dirt road to your right is Old Santa Elena Road, a mostly hard-packed downhill easy 14-mile ride. An alternate route is to continue on pavement for 7 miles to paved Castolon-Santa Elena Road. It's then 22 miles to Castolon campground and another 8 miles to Santa Elena Canyon campground. Here you'll see the 1,500-foot cliff on the Terlingua Fault Scarp towering from the edge of the river.

Day 4 — *Santa Elena to primitive camping along the River Road — 30 miles.* The road is paved to Castolon, where there is an old trading post now a store, a ranger station, and a nearby campground. If you plan to use the River Road, be sure to get a wilderness permit from the ranger here. And make sure that you get water! River Road leaves pavement 3 miles north of Castolon. Then it's another 51 miles to Boquillas Canyon Road. All vehicles stopped to give us water, but have plenty on hand as there is usually not much traffic. You can camp anywhere, anytime along the river or in the desert.

Day 5 — *River Road to Rio Grande Village — 37 miles.* River Road becomes paved road about five miles before Boquillas Canyon and Rio Grande Village. The village has a store, showers, laundry, and campground. There is a Hot Springs turnoff before the downhill to the village. The Boquillas Canyon route is an eight-mile round trip and two-mile hike round trip to the mouth of the canyon.

Days 4 and 5—Alternate to the River Road. From Castolon continue on pavement back to the main park road and on to the Chisos Basin campground. This is a hilly 45 miles. To Boquillas it is 30 miles downhill.

Day 6 — Rio Grande Village to the Chisos Basin — 30 miles. About 20 miles of gradual climbing leads to Panther Junction and park headquarters. You will continue climbing toward the Chisos Basin until the last mile or so which is a fast drop. This gets you into the mountain terrain of the park, with a lodge, motel, campground, and store.

Day 7 — The Basin to Green Valley via Highway 118 — 66 miles. Climb back up and over Panther Pass, 5,800 feet, and exit the park at Maverick and Study Butte, 2,800 feet. There is a store here and water is available. Take Highway 118 north toward Alpine. After some climbing, you'll see Green Valley spread below you. An old dirt road will get you off of the highway.

Day 8 — Green Valley to Marfa via Highway 118 and U.S. 90 — 70 miles. This stretch does more climbing than dropping, Alpine being at 4,485 feet and Marfa a bit higher. Camping is available at Woodward Ranch, 2 miles off 118 and 15 miles before Alpine. Go west on U.S. 90 to Marfa with a "shoulder" and a tail wind.

Notes

Yellowstone-Grand Teton: Five-Day Tour

Location
Tours in the Yellowstone-Grand Teton area are characterized by great scenery and wildlife appeal. This particular bicycle tour begins in Livingston, Montana, which can be reached by Amtrak (service three times a week), and ends in Idaho Falls, Idaho. From this point you can take a bus to Pocatello, Idaho (daily service), and catch the next train back to your home.

Season
We traveled the route in the summer, when the parks were having their peak seasons. Therefore, we always started riding as early as possible to beat the afternoon heat and traffic. We also arrived at our overnight destinations about 3 P.M. to avoid the traditional late afternoon thunderstorms of these regions.

Accommodations
Campsites are frequent along the way. Be sure to secure campsite reservations within Yellowstone and Grand Teton by writing to the parks. Food is available at all projected destinations with breakfast never more than five miles down the road.

Level of Difficulty
This is a five-day tour of moderate difficulty totaling 320 miles. We found the ride to be an absolute pleasure that required only a moderate pace. The terrain is fairly hilly, but many mountain plateaus offer hours of pleasurable freewheeling with ample time for sightseeing, photographing, and meeting people.

References

For the most thorough maps of the area, contact Yellowstone Park Co., WY 82190, and Grand Teton National Park, Moose, WY 83012.

Tour Outline and Points of Interest

Day 1 — Livingston, Montana, to Gardiner — 54 miles. Arriving by Amtrak, check your watch. If you have at least six hours of daylight remaining and no troublesome south wind, get your gear together and expect a beautifully level and smooth Highway 89 to Gardiner. This ride presents the Big Sky country at its best.

If you need snacks for the five-hour ride you can shop at the supermarket on your way out of town.

Gardiner is a full-service town with ample private campgrounds, lodging, and a fine restaurant. Be sure to purchase your riding snacks for tomorrow before retiring.

If you arrive late you have an alternate escape to Gardiner via the Yellowstone Bus Lines 4 P.M. run. They'll pick up you and your boxed bike at the train landing; however you'll have to walk about three blocks to the bus depot, purchase a $3.05 ticket and let them know that you'll be waiting at the train station.

Day 2 — Gardiner to Old Faithful — 56 miles. Get up early! The local restaurant opens at 6 A.M. and you'll want an early start. Try to be through the Yellowstone gateway by 7 A.M. The ranger will collect 50¢ from each rider.

Climbing alongside the Gardiner River you'll encounter about eight miles of uphill before leveling off a mile beyond the Mammoth Hot Springs complex. We maintained a steady but easy pace and arrived at the top about 2½ hours later. From here to the Madison junction you will experience a great variety of wonders that include all types of bubbling hot springs, meadows, wetlands, creatures of many descriptions, snow-capped peaks, geological phenomena, and mosquitos that will demand a repellent.

Lunch is on your own as you continue alongside the Gibbon River. I suggest you take a rest stop at the Madison complex before you start the rather testy uphill just beyond. Once you've conquered gravity at this location it's a beautiful downhill ride toward Old Faithful. We arrived around 4 P.M. and just managed to beat the usual afternoon thunderstorms.

Our overnight at the big geyser was memorable. We had reservations for a budget shelter that put a roof over our heads for a mere $10.40. Along with the spectacular fountain we found Old Faithful Inn to be a real journey back to the style of early-day lodging. On the

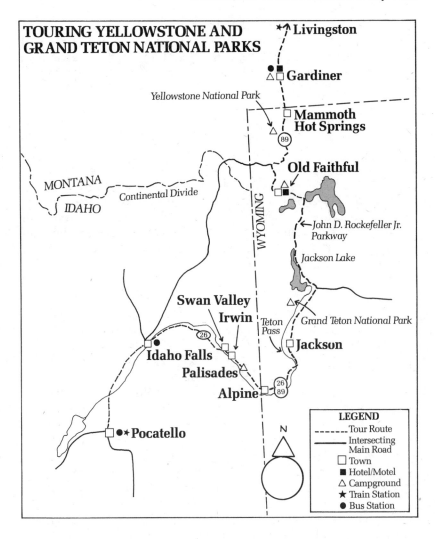

TOURING YELLOWSTONE AND GRAND TETON NATIONAL PARKS

Livingston

Gardiner

Yellowstone National Park

Mammoth Hot Springs

89

MONTANA

Continental Divide

IDAHO

WYOMING

Old Faithful

←John D. Rockefeller Jr. Parkway

Jackson Lake

Swan Valley

Irwin

Teton Pass

Grand Teton National Park

26

Idaho Falls

Palisades

Alpine

Jackson

26
89

N

Pocatello

LEGEND
------- Tour Route
——— Intersecting Main Road
☐ Town
■ Hotel/Motel
△ Campground
★ Train Station
● Bus Station

minus side you can expect high prices, amateur service, and poor food at the commercial establishments.

Purchase ample provisions for tomorrow's ride because it will require a high energy output.

Day 3 — Old Faithful to Colter Bay — 61 miles. Breakfast is at 6 A.M. at the Snow Lodge on your way out of the park.

Today you will meet the Continental Divide on three occasions, however no severe gear-grinding will be necessary. The roadway is excellent and the quiet and solitude during the early morning hours

57

provide a great experience. The third crossing is almost unnotice-able and the remaining 18 miles to the south entrance of the park is a downhill ride along the Lewis River Canyon. The Lewis Falls scenic overlook is congested so be defensive and avoid that run-down feeling.

This southern portion of the park differs considerably in that the scenery seems a bit less programmed. Expect heavy traffic south of West Thumb as you pedal the only existing roadway toward the Grand Tetons.

Upon leaving Yellowstone you will enter the John D. Rockefeller Jr. Parkway. This land was purchased by Rockefeller and deeded to the National Park System as a preserved link between the two parks. After seven miles of rather uneventful travel you will enter the Teton north entrance and encounter some rolling roadway until you end the day at the Colter Bay Village campground.

John Colter was the first settler in this region, and the sunset on the Tetons as you gaze across Jackson Lake from your campsite is testimony to his good judgment.

Colter Bay is a full-service campground and culminated a day that found us early to bed after a challenging but satisfying journey.

Day 4 — Colter Bay to Palisades — 97 miles. On this day we climbed out at 4:30 A.M., fixed a quick breakfast, and started a ride that will rival any part of this world in beauty and majesty. If you prefer, breakfast can be found about five miles down the road at Jackson Lake Lodge, but it was still closed as we cruised in the early morning sunrise. Now you begin to realize why you took this tour. A beautiful bike shoulder on level roadway appears as you bear right at the Jackson Lake junction.

These Grand Tetons, rightfully named by a homesick French-man, present a panorama that is a setting of solitude and natural wonder. At North Jenny Lake junction we chose the straight road to the south junction, but I understand that the Jenny Lake campground offers a spectacular sight with the mountains rising directly out of the lake surface.

As we approached the Moose Entrance station and made our exit of the Teton area I couldn't help but notice that the roadside vegetation had a head wind bend to it. We may have missed a struggle to Jackson because of our early start.

As you enter this tourist haven try to catch the first restaurant on the right side of the road. It has a low profile with plenty of parked cars out front, along with superior food, good service, and a com-fortable atmosphere.

Jackson has an excellent cycle shop so if you have any needs you're going to get satisfaction. Incidentally, if you're there on July

4 you may wish to get involved in their annual 100-mile loop race that carries you over 9,000-foot Teton Pass. Our legs told us to pass on this event.

Take Highway 26-89 and enjoy a comfortable afternoon ride to Alpine junction. It started to get very warm here so we rested a couple of hours and then set out for the KOA campground about 25 miles distant, just beyond the Palisades Dam. This is an earthen monster that will have you praying for deliverance from any earthly tremors during the night. The owner offered to sell us the place.

Day 5 — Palisades to Idaho Falls — 51 miles. Just a couple of level miles south is the community of Irwin. Expect a nice tail wind and catch breakfast at the local cafe. Continuing on you'll enjoy the Swan Valley and the Snake River that accompanies you along this portion of the tour.

Now it's time to pay the dues. As you climb out of the river canyon and hit the level there is evidence of a very strong side wind. Then as you gradually bear in a more westerly direction expect to encounter a head wind that turns the remaining eight miles into a marathon battle. Expect this to happen and plan accordingly; it's a daily expectation in this region. Four mph was about the best we could manage.

After arriving at Idaho Falls in a semi-stupor we gradually regained our senses and promptly decided to abort the remaining 46 miles of hurricane winds that howled between us and our anticipated destination of Pocatello.

We located the bus depot and solved our bike box problem by going to Bill's Bike Shop about two blocks from the bus station. Here we found some discarded bike boxes and packing up, we boarded the 3 P.M. bus and bid farewell to the wind and dust that constituted the scenery thereabouts and all the way to Pocatello.

Our luck returned as we entered Pocatello and found the bus and train depots about 50 yards apart. We treated ourselves to a fine dinner, got involved in a great jam session at the Bistro on South Main, caught the 3:30 A.M. Pioneer Limited and arrived in Seattle on schedule at 9:30 P.M. the same day.

Notes

Cycling in the Promised Land

Location

This is a two-week, 740-mile tour of five National Parks (Canyonlands, Arches, Capitol Reef, Bryce Canyon, Zion), Natural Bridges National Monument, and Dead Horse Point State Park. The tour begins in Green River, Utah, and ends in St. George, Utah.

Logistics are very tricky. Ours were complicated to say the least. One member rode down from Salt Lake City, one was driven by friends from Denver, others drove. It would be easier to make a loop, especially if only one week is available for the tour. You'd see the first three parks and monument. Green River is served by bus and the Denver Rio Grande Railroad, which wants to do away with passenger service on the Utah portion and wouldn't load one bike in Denver but did another in Grand Junction. So the railroad is very tenuous. St. George has bus and air service (via Las Vegas and Salt Lake City). There are bike shops there to get a box, needed for the bus. If flying, go via Grand Junction and take I-70 west, then Route 128 to Arches and follow the route from there.

If driving, it's about 50 miles back to Green River from Hanksville (Day 8). One person went back, picked up the vehicle, drove to Zion, and cycled back toward the group. If only one week is available, then looping back to Green River makes a good tour.

Season

Mid-May to November is the best time to make this trip. It snowed the week before we started riding on May 13. Then spring just burst forth each day as we proceeded along the route, absolutely perfect timing for flowers and color. In the early morning (6 A.M.) temperatures ranged from 30° to 58° F. Day temperatures ranged from 45° to 90° F., so be prepared with appropriate clothing.

60

Accommodations

This is strictly a camping tour, and we camped at times along the road when we didn't make the intended destination. Highway patrol are very helpful, and they didn't seem to mind our using the roadside rest areas. Bryce Canyon and Zion have tourist facilities; the others don't.

Level of Difficulty

This is a wilderness tour with open space on paved roads (mostly) and very little traffic to contend with. You can cover as much or as little mileage per day as you want, but you must be willing to carry food and water. Services are sparse. The first three parks don't even have electricity, telephones, accommodations, stores, or snack bars.

References

Superintendent, Canyonlands and Arches National Parks, Moab, UT 84532; Superintendent, Capitol Reef National Park, Torrey, UT 84775; Superintendent, Bryce Canyon National Park, Bryce Canyon, UT 84717; Superintendent, Zion National Park, Springdale, UT 84767. Phone (801) 772-3256; Glen Canyon National Recreation Area, Box 1507, Page, AZ 86040.

For topographic maps, USGS—Distribution, Central Region, Denver Federal Center, Bldg. 41, Denver, CO 80225; National Park Service Public Information, 125 S. State St., Salt Lake City, UT 84114. Phone (801) 524-4165.

For regional maps, Utah Travel Council, Council Hall, Salt Lake City, UT 84114. Phone (801) 533-5681 (request maps 1, 2, and 5); Arizona Highways, 2039 W. Lewis Ave., Phoenix, AZ 85009.

For services and accommodations, Chamber of Commerce, 88 N. Main St., Monticello, UT 84534.

Tour Outline and Points of Interest

Day 1 — Green River, Utah (4,079 feet) to Dead Horse Point State Park (6,000 feet) — 65 miles. Go east on I-70 to Crescent Junction where there is a gas station. Turn right on 163 to Canyonlands National Park, take turnoff 313 and turn right. Proceed on 313 to Dead Horse, a basically uphill route with one especially steep climb. About a mile in from the junction are pleasant lunch spots under large trees, next to a small stream. You could make dry camp anywhere along the route, but you would have to carry in enough water and food as there are no services or water after leaving the town in Green River. There is water at the campground and ice at the visitors' center. Camping is $5 a site. It's another mile out to the spectacular overlook, and 2,000 feet below the meandering Colorado River flows, cutting forever deeper into the canyons. This is a grand view of the national park at sunset or sunrise. I seemed to get better color contrast in photographs in the morning, with the moon in the background.

Day 2 — Dead Horse Point State Park (6,000 feet) to Moab (4,000 feet — 30 miles. To go into Canyonlands National Park proper, you must retrace eight miles to The Knoll and take a dirt road into the park. There is a campground at Green River overlook (get verification about available water at the ranger station and campground). You can then drop to the Colorado River via Shafter Trail (also dirt) and then follow the paved scenic Highway 279 into Moab. Our choice was one of shorter distance but perhaps no less challenging or spectacular. From the campground retrace approximately six miles on pavement and turn right onto a prominent dirt road (Long Canyon) heading directly toward La Sal Mountains. This starts as a wide graded dirt road on a fairly gently downhill then drops into a very steep, narrow, one track canyon trail for several miles, then emerges into wider canyons and a less steep descent to the river. Because of the steepness of this route, most people walked different portions but commented that the scenery was worth it. Turn left when you reach pavement and the river, 2,000 feet lower now, and go on Moab via scenic Highway 279. The only decent camping spot that we saw was under some trees on the left (road going in) right after the Dinosaur Rock sign. The river is very silty this time of year so it is questionable as drinking water. If you turn right at the junction with pavement and ride a couple miles, you'll come to Potash mining operation (seen from Dead Horse Point). You could possibly get water there.

Moab has trailer parks with campsites/showers and laundry, cost $6-$7 per site, for two, then 75¢ for each additional person. There are free campsites along the Colorado River on 128 east of Moab, but there are no showers. You'll also find a bike shop in Moab.

Day 3 — Moab (4,000 feet) to Devil's Garden Campground (5,355 feet) in Arches National Park — 38 miles. From Moab go north on 163 to Arches headquarters and visitor center. Entrance is free for cyclists. You can take an optional turnoff for the Windows section of the park. Proceed on the main road to Devil's Garden area (en route optional turnoff for Delicate Arch). The rangers are extremely pleasant here and assured us if we had arrived to find the campground full, they would have made space for us somewhere. Cost of the site is $3.

Day 4 — Devil's Garden Campground (5,355 feet) to Church Rock (6,000 feet) — 67 miles. Retrace to the entrance to Arches National Park, then turn left on 163 to Moab. From Moab continue on 163 to La Sal Junction; en route there's a nice roadside rest on the left with restrooms, shade trees, grass, and water. La Sal Junction has two gas stations and a cafe. From Moab, the road starts as a gentle river grade up, then becomes a steeper climb to La Sal Junction. From La Sal Junction proceed to Church Rock at the junction with 211. If you feel up to it, you could continue on 211 to Newspaper Rock State Park where there is a pleasant campground and impressive petroglyphs.

Day 5 — Church Rock (6,000 feet) to Blanding (6,400 feet) — 41 miles. Back at the 163/211 junction, turn right (south) to Monticello. This is mostly uphill but there are some nice camping places among the pinion pines and small stream. Monticello (7,100 feet) has motels, stores, a small visitor center, and museum. Monticello to Devil's Canyon forest service campground is a steep down then up. Devil's Canyon to Blanding is another steep down and up. There is a trailer park on the south side of town with good showers, about $1.25 per person. Cedars State Historical and Indian (Anasazi) Cultural Museum is new and has excellent displays; it is well worth the visit.

Day 6 — Blanding (6,400 feet) to Natural Bridges National Monument (6,500 feet) — 51 miles. From Blanding proceed to the junction of 95. Highway 95 is a recent accomplishment of the Utah Department of Transportation and is truly a magnificent road for riding with smooth wide lanes and shoulders and no traffic to speak of. Warning: from Blanding to Hanksville, 120 miles, there are no services available except water at Natural Bridges, Fry Canyon, and Hite Marina. Food can be found at Fry Canyon (very minimal and mostly snack food) and Hite Marina (fairly good selection, no fresh vegetables or fruits, though). At the junction, take 95 to Natural Bridges turnoff. En route there's a long drop through Comb Ridge followed by a 10-mile uphill climb (steepest at the bottom). Here you'll find Mule Canyon Ruins with a rest area (no water), and well-preserved Anasazi Indian ruins over 700 years old. From the Natural Bridges turnoff go to the visitors' center where there is no charge for bikes. Water is available at the center, but none at the nearby campground. Take the Bridges loop road through the monument with trails down to the three natural bridges: Sipapu, Kachina, and Owachomo; these are well worth exploring, especially by hiking if you have the time.

Day 7 — Natural Bridges (6,500 feet) to Hog Springs Picnic Area on 95 (4,700 feet)—54 miles. This is a downhill day with the first 50 miles ridden in three hours. Ride from Natural Bridges to Fry Canyon where there is a meager store with water that opens at 8 A.M. Then cycle from Fry Canyon to Hite Marina where there's a store, water, campground, and lots of boaters. From Hite Marina travel to Hog Springs Rest Area. There are a few access spots to the lake for swimming, and it's a steep uphill away from the lake then a gentle downhill to North Wash, which may be silty this time of year but there are several good spots to sit in the river to cool off. At Hog Springs follow the trail a short ways up the canyon and find a pool and spring for bathing.

Day 8 — Hog Springs (4,700 feet) to Capitol Reef National Park (5,400 feet) — 76 miles. Hog Springs to Hanksville is an easy uphill grade. Turn left on 24 to Caineville, an easy river grade up with a beautiful valley and pastures. Proceed from Caineville to River Ford, which is not a town as such, but is a good place to get into the Fremont River for a clean, cool dip. You'll next come to the Capitol Reef entrance where there is no charge. There are many scenic viewpoints along the way to the campground where you'll find water, tables, and bathrooms but no showers, all for $2 per site.

Day 9 — Capitol Reef (5,400 feet) to Koosharem Rest Area (8,000 feet) — 43 miles. This is an uphill day with a tremendous head wind all the way. There is a steep climb from Capitol Reef Park to Torre where you'll find a store, cafe, and trailer park. Farther on you'll encounter Bicknell and a store, cafe, motel, and campground before the town. Continue on through Lyman and Loa and reach Summit (8,406 feet) where there is a roadside rest, water, tables, and pit toilets. Services are available in Koosharem, two miles away.

Day 10 — Koosharem Rest Area (8,000 feet) to Panguitch (6,670 feet) — 80 miles. Go back uphill about ¼ mile, turn right on the road which becomes dirt and follow to the town of Koosharem, left on Highway 62. Koosharem to Otter Creek Campground is an easy downhill into a valley to a beautiful lakeside camp with hot showers. Continue on 62 to Kingston (no services) and then left on Highway 89 to Circleville. Circleville to Panguitch is an upward river grade and here there are services, KOA, and motels.

Recommended Optional Route to Bryce. From Otter Creek Campground proceed to Antimony (store and water); continue on this road to where the pavement ends and the sign says 38 miles to Bryce. The road is loose rock at first and follows the Sevier River in flood stage at this time. The route begins to climb at Orisis and becomes hard-packed uphill for about two miles. Then you'll reach a big flat plateau. A seven-mile stretch here is paved, then becomes hard dirt again through Emery Valley to junction of Highway 12 and entrance to Bryce Canyon.

Day 11 — Panguitch (6,670 feet) to Bryce Canyon entrance (7,586 feet) — 36 miles. Leave Panguitch on Highway 89 to the junction with 12. Turn left on 12 to Bryce entrance which is mostly an uphill route. Red Canyon Campground is along a stream here. Foster's Bakery is at the top of the hill and there is a small store.

Optional rides in the park itself: from visitor center to Bryce Point, semicircle around Bryce Amphitheater, includes Sunset Point, Inspiration Point, and then Bryce Point; to Rainbow Point includes Fairview Point, Natural Bridge, Aqua Canyon, and Rainbow Point at 9,105 feet.

Day 12 — Bryce Canyon (7,586 feet) to Mt. Carmel Trailer Park (6,000 feet) — 59 miles. Go west on 12, then left on 89 to Hatch with its store, cafe, and motel. From Hatch ride to Long Valley Junction, summit 7,700 feet, which is an easy uphill river grade and there's a store at the top. From Long Valley proceed to Glendale (store, motel, rest area) and then onto Orderville (store, campground) and from Orderville to Mt. Carmel Trailer Park.

Day 13 — Mt. Carmel (6,000 feet) to Zion National Park (4,000 feet) — 34 miles. From the trailer park proceed to the junction with 9, Mt. Carmel Junction. Turn right on 9 to National Park Visitor Center, which involves some easy climbing at first, then an exhilarating downhill into the park. Caution: there are two tunnels, the first is short and easy to pass through, but the second one is one mile long and very black; stop a car for escort through or ask a ranger at the entrance. After the tunnel it's a fantastic zigzag downhill to the valley floor with the visitors' center and two campgrounds nearby.

Day 14 — Zion National Park (4,000 feet) to St. George (2,880 feet) — *41 miles*. Go west on Highway 9 to the junction with 17 (passes a few small towns), then left on 9 to the Harrisburg junction and left to Washington. Take I-15 to the St. George exit where you'll find an airport and bus services to take you to your home destination.

Notes

Arizona Deserts
and Forests Tour

Location

Here is a tour ideal for anyone; along its course the beautiful diversity of Arizona is revealed as the route leads out of the desert up into the tall pine forests.

The tour begins in the old mining town of Cave Creek, 15 miles north of Phoenix. Cave Creek is over 100 years old. It was once a mining settlement in the foothills, a stagecoach stop, and later a stopover for city folk on their way to the two lakes just northeast of Cave Creek (accessible only by a 12-mile-long dirt road).

More recently Cave Creek has become somewhat of an arts and crafts center where several fairs are held each year under the tamarack trees. The big one, usually in March, also hosts a parade and rodeo.

Season

This tour is most pleasant in late spring or late summer. Though it can be done in mid-summer and offers a nice retreat from the desert heat, preparations and care must be taken for riding in the intense heat of the desert lowlands. Even in the higher elevations, though not as hot, the sun is more intense and a good sunscreen is needed.

During the summer afternoons, thunderstorms are common in the northern mountains. They usually begin about July 1 and continue through the end of August. Clouds usually begin to build around noon and rain may fall later in the day or at night. Or the clouds may be pushed around you, depending on the terrain. Normally the storms last no more than a couple of hours, a day at the most.

Also, summer is the time of year when rattlesnakes and other poisonous crawlers come out. Be careful when you walk, especially along the creeks and in rocky areas. Scorpions like the warmth under bedrolls and tents.

Accommodations

Campgrounds and motels are frequent along this entire route, so you can make this strictly a camping tour, strictly a motel tour, or a combination of both.

Level of Difficulty

Depending on your pace and amount of leisure time, this tour takes about a week. I have traveled this route in both directions and find the clockwise trip to be the easiest in relation to the mountain climbs. Traffic conditions vary throughout the route, ranging from moderate to a bit heavier around the larger towns.

References

Because this tour travels fairly major routes, an adequate state map of Arizona is the most helpful. You may also want to write to the National Forests, Prescott and Tonto, for their available tourist information.

Tour Outline and Points of Interest

From Cave Creek head south on Cave Creek Road, which winds around Black Mountain, and turn west at the stop sign (Carefree Highway). Fifteen miles of level road (one small hill) leads to a grocery store at the intersection of Interstate 17. This is a good place to refresh and refuel, since the next town is 40 miles away. The land is flat most of the way, except for a several mile downhill and climb out of the Pleasant Valley.

This is perhaps the quietest section of this tour, as there is little traffic on this road. And the road has a wide paved shoulder. In the distance on either side are jagged purple mountains.

About five miles before Wickenburg there is a roadside stop for picnic or camping. This is along the Hassayampa River which usually runs only in the spring.

From Wickenburg, past the historic Vulture Gold Mine, the desert road rises slightly for ten miles before reaching the ghost town (almost) of Congress. Some of the people here are miners who work in the local hills where gold is mined even today. I wouldn't suggest venturing on your own to find a mine; most of them are on private land.

As you sit in Congress, take time to refresh and gain strength.

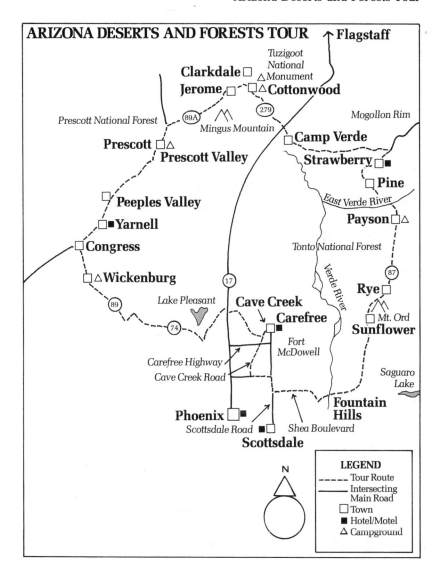

The hill to Yarnell is clearly visible as it looms just outside of town, a nine-mile climb up to where "the desert sun meets the mountain breeze." The road is four-lane divided highway with occasional cars and trucks. It is an older, rougher road, but the view is exhilarating!

At the summit is the quiet town of Yarnell, on the edge of a fertile green valley. Yarnell is a small town with a few motels, two grocery stores, and a fountain in honor of St. Joseph where you are invited to stop and have a drink of cool spring water. There is also a park among the trees for camping.

Outside Yarnell, cattle graze on the lush green of the Peeples Valley.

Then suddenly the land becomes barren rock and prairie for several miles before rising into the pines of Prescott. It is 30 miles from Yarnell to Prescott, about 13 miles of rolling uphills through the Prescott National Forest. Though it is mostly uphill, with little traffic, there are several sweeping downhills also.

Just before Prescott there is a state park ($3 fee) which may be full by midday during the July 4 season. And there are plenty of motels just as you enter town. A good place to take a day off may be this day of the tour. There are two good bicycle shops in Prescott for needed parts and repairs.

Prescott has as many festivities as it does cracks in its aged roads. Every July 4 one of the largest rodeos in the state is held here, but beware of the drivers as they tend to be pretty wild. Be sure to go by the old Santa Fe train station near the grassy town square.

Heading out of Prescott, the road drops through the "Granite Dells," odd rock formations, then heads east on Highway 69 across the plains of the Prescott Valley. Ten miles from this town is a gas station at the entrance to the community of Prescott Valley.

The ten-mile ride of Mingus Mountain is a lovely, winding climb. There is little traffic, only an occasional car or truck. At the summit is a restaurant that appears to open only at night during the skiing season. There is a short downhill, then a climb, then just around the turn, an awesome view! The San Francisco Peaks of Flagstaff can be seen far off in the distance, just in front are the Red Rocks of Sedona, and below is the lush green of the Verde Valley.

The winding road out of the pines along rocky cliffs is over-whelming; the speed can become so fast. I had to stop several times to let slow-moving recreational vehicles speed up enough to get ahead and to regain my composure.

About halfway down the mountain, you suddenly enter the ghost town of Jerome. Once a mining town that housed 10,000 people, this cliffhanger has a few residents, more so since becoming a tourist attraction. There is a museum (actually the whole town is somewhat of a museum) and several food and gift shops. It is interesting to walk through this town and inspect the nooks and crannies.

The road descends faster into Clarkdale, which could easily be passed by if you are one who hates to stop in the middle of a nice coast. Off to the left is the cement plant where most of the local cement is produced.

Then into Cottonwood, a much larger town, which has an excellent place for camping on the south side of town. Just across the river is Dead Horse State Park, where for $3 you can camp and shower in modern facilities. At night the lights up at Jerome look like twinkling stars.

Also in this area is Tuzigoot National Monument where Indian dwellings of old still partially remain.

From here it is 12 miles to the once Calvary post of Camp Verde, now mostly a farming and retirement community along the Verde River.

Running parallel to Route 87 out of Camp Verde, the road crosses the river and begins to climb along the General Crook Trail. The road parallels the rugged trail used by the Calvary in the 1800s. Altogether it is about 45 miles to the next town, half of which is uphill as you climb into the pine-covered ridge of the Mogollon Rim. But it is a gradual incline on a wide road with a grand view of the rim to the right. The road meets Route 87, where you go right. (To the left is Flagstaff, via Happy Jack and Lake Mary.) Once in the trees, it is all downhill, through switchbacks, into Strawberry. This is a favorite honeymoon resort with a hotel, grocery store, gas station, and—this is its boast—"the only bar in Arizona with an elevator."

The next town is five miles down the road and is appropriately called Pine. Larger than Strawberry, Pine is home for many valley residents seeking refuge from the summer heat. There are several grocery stores and a couple of short-order restaurants.

Six miles south of Pine is the largest known travertine bridge, a natural wonder of rock that spans Pine Creek. The bridge was discovered in 1877 by David Gowan who found refuge from the Indians high on a ledge in the tunnel. He stayed hidden for three days before climbing out and claiming squatter's rights over both the bridge and five fertile acres. He moved on, but not before securing his find with his nephew from Scotland whose family came to farm the land around the turn of the century. They also built a lodge which still stands and houses tourists.

Go through the picnic grounds and hike along the river through the trees that lead to the bridge, a truly awesome spectacle.

Ten miles farther there is a campsite along the East Verde River with a swimming hole and rocky cliffs for exploring. This spot is only four miles outside of Payson, the last actual town before dropping out of the pines and down to the desert.

Payson is similar to Prescott in many ways, though smaller. It hosts a lumberjack festival and fiddlers' convention, along with several bluegrass and arts and crafts festivals during the spring through autumn months.

The long, lazy downhills lead back to the valley, with one long climb at Mt. Ord (7,155 feet) where the road crosses the Mazatal Range. This road is fairly busy, being the only route from Phoenix to Payson.

Near Sunflower the road narrows and snakes along the tree-lined Sycamore Creek. The town of Sunflower hides 36 miles from Payson. All I ever saw was a farm and a bar and grill that sits off the main road a few hundred yards at the end of a dirt road. It is easy to miss this place since there are no official markings.

Desert vegetation gradually begins to appear. Twenty miles from Sunflower is the turnoff to Saguaro Lake where boating and camping are popular. This is a canyon lake with sheer rocky walls.

Ten miles farther you cross the Verde River at Fort McDowell. Then only ten more miles where you turn west (right) onto Shea Boulevard. It's a long stretch of rather barren road down from Payson, but that's all behind now.

At Fountain Hills there is a modern restaurant and an information center to lure prospective land buyers to this new town.

The road into Scottsdale is wide with an ample shoulder for riding. To the left is an excellent view of downtown Phoenix. Once in Scottsdale, take a right on Scottsdale Road, which heads north along the Foothills Scenic Drive, past Rawhide, a collection of arts and crafts shops with an Old West appearance. The next town you will hit will be Carefree.

In Carefree, aside from elaborate houses, there is a grocery store, souvenir shops and several restaurants. Home of the world's largest sundial and several famous people, Carefree lives up to its name.

At Carefree, Scottsdale Road becomes Tom Darlington Drive, named in honor of one of the founders of Carefree. Tom Darlington Drive meets Cave Creek Road which leads through Cave Creek and completes the loop.

Notes

Valley Center, California Loop

Location

This 115-mile loop tour starts and ends in Valley Center, California, which is northeast of Escondido and San Diego. Public transportation to Valley Center is lacking. For this reason, the tour can start from Oceanside and go in reverse, as Amtrak is available there. Amtrak service also runs to San Diego, and there is an airport in that city.

Season

Spring and fall are the ideal times to tour this area as fruits are in season and there are plenty of fresh fruit stands along the route. But you can cycle this loop virtually any time of year.

Accommodations

This is a camping tour, starting and ending at Woods Valley Campground in Valley Center.

Level of Difficulty

This short loop provides a nice variety of the hill country of San Diego County, its seashore, and the gradual drop and climb in between the two.

References

Use the Caltrans District 11 Bicycling Map, P.O. Box 81406, San Diego, CA 92138. It's free.

Tour Outline and Points of Interest

Day 1 — Woods Valley Campground to La Jolla Indian Camp

73

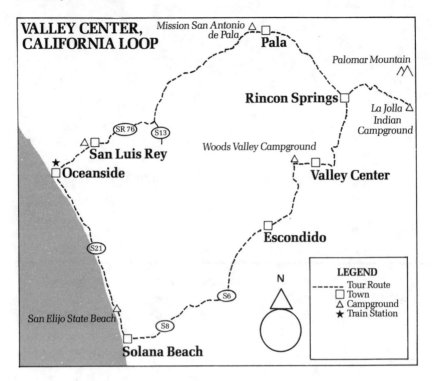

VALLEY CENTER, CALIFORNIA LOOP

Mission San Antonio de Pala

Pala

Palomar Mountain

Rincon Springs

La Jolla Indian Campground

SR 76   S13

Woods Valley Campground

San Luis Rey

Oceanside

Valley Center

Escondido

S21

N

LEGEND
------- Tour Route
□ Town
△ Campground
★ Train Station

San Elijo State Beach

S6

S8

Solana Beach

2. Turn left on Woods Valley Road, left on Lake Wohlford Road toward Rincon Springs. Go right on Valley Center Road and S6 toward Palomar Mountain. At the junction of SR 76 (Rincon Springs), turn right following S6 and SR 76 east. There is a store up this hill. At the junction turnoff for Palomar Mountain, follow SR 76 toward Lake Henshaw. La Jolla Indian Camp 1 is on your right. La Jolla Indian Camp 2 is also on your right, this one having less of a hill to climb. It is on the river with primitive camping and outhouses available. You must obtain permission from the Indian in charge to stay here. San Luis Rey campground is a short distance farther down the road, and there are also camping facilities at Lake Henshaw.

A good side trip on this day's tour is up Palomar Mountain, 6,140 feet, to the world famous observatory. The east grade up Palomar is less steep than the western one. There is a campground on this route also.

Day 2 — La Jolla Camp 2 to San Elijo State Beach. From La Jolla Camp 2 retrace your route (downhill) to Rincon Springs. In 8.9 miles you will find a junction with S6. Bear right and follow SR 76 toward Oceanside. The junction with I-15 is at mile 25.3 and there is a market on your right. At Pala the traffic noticeably picks up and there are no ridable shoulders. Mission San Antonio de Pala is a very interesting side trip and there is a campground nearby.

At mile 30.1, turn left following SR 76 and S13 toward Oceanside. There are fruit stands all along here. Take a right after the bridge and cycle SR 76 to Oceanside. Before entering Oceanside, you pass by Mission San Luis Rey.

You will be on Hill Street in Oceanside. Turn left onto Cleveland Street, right onto Hill Street and S21. At mile 58.2 you will be at San Elijo State Beach. San Elijo State Beach has a bike/hike campsite where you can stay for 50¢; no reservations necessary.

Day 3 — San Elijo State Beach to Woods Valley Campground. Leave the park and turn right (south) on S21. This route continues to follow the shoreline. Turn left on S8 at Solana Beach. This passes under I-15, then by San Dieguito County Park, which is worth a short rest stop visit. Next turn right on S6 toward Lake Hodges and Escondido. S6 becomes Valley Parkway which passes under I-15. Bear right onto one-way 2nd Avenue, which leads back onto two-way Valley Parkway S6. Turn right onto Woods Valley Road.

Notes

Joshua Tree
National Monument Loop

Location

This fabulous 170-mile bicycle trip takes off from Indio, California, at 15 feet below sea level and proceeds from low to high desert (the highest point is Salton View at 5,185 feet above sea level), and descends again by way of Box Canyon, Salton Sea, Mecca, and date gardens back to the starting point in Indio.

Featured are urban sprawl, beautiful planned communities, colorful rock formations, shifting sand, yucca plants, Joshua trees, desert tortoises, lizards, birds, a wide variety of cacti, an oasis or two, and in April or early May, a magnificent array of wildflowers.

Indio is a natural starting point because of its location on routes from both northern and southern California. Amtrak makes Sunday, Tuesday, and Friday stops from Los Angeles, but recently ceased to carry bikes because of abandonment of baggage service there.

Season

Desert nights in the higher altitudes are cold in winter, and the summer is unbearably hot. Winter also brings the possibility of rain. April and May are wildflower times that provide the maximum attraction. During any time of year, severe sandstorms can occur. This is a risk that should be considered.

Accommodations

This tour is primarily planned around camping facilities within Joshua Tree National Monument, though motels are available in Indio. Ace Campground (private) in Indio gives a royal welcome to bicyclists. It is located at 82-815 Avenue 42, Indio, CA 92201, a few yards north of Jackson Street. From the center of town, head north on Jackson Street and as the freeway overpass gives an elevated view,

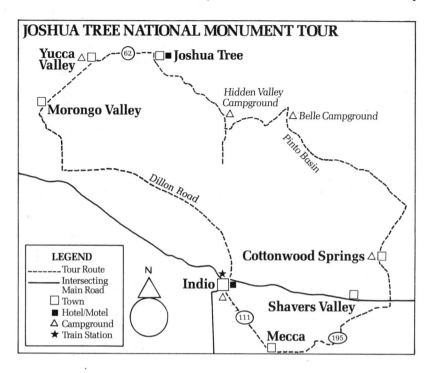

JOSHUA TREE NATIONAL MONUMENT TOUR

it is possible to see the Ace Campground sign several blocks ahead on the left.

Level of Difficulty

All the roads on this loop are well paved. The roads within the Monument are two-lane oil and gravel with adequate shoulders in most places. Some surfaces have sharp gravel and a washboard effect, and sew-up tires could be vulnerable. A medium level of tourist traffic is to be expected with a liberal sprinkling of recreational vehicles. Generally speaking, the first half of the trip is climbing and the second half is downhill. For the most part the grades are quite bearable. It is recommended that the loop be ridden clockwise, because of the desirability of descending Box Canyon on the southern portion. It can become a fiery furnace, especially in the afternoons.

Within the Monument, water is a problem. A collapsible water bottle, or bottles, with a total capacity of at least a gallon should be a part of each cyclist's equipment. This amounts to approximately 10 pounds of extra weight, but it is necessary for survival.

Tour Outline and Points of Interest

Day 1 — Indio to Hidden Valley Campground. In Indio, turn east on Avenue 44 from Jackson Street to Dillon Road, then left on Dillon Road to Indian Avenue, right on Indian Avenue to California Highway 62, and finally right on 62 to the town of Morongo Valley. Continue on 62 to the town of Joshua Tree.

At this point, 60 miles have been traversed. The options are: stop before Joshua Tree and turn off right just beyond the town of Yucca Valley about 3.5 miles south of 62 to Yogi Bear's Jellystone Campground (private); take a motel in the town of Joshua Tree; or proceed through the town of Joshua Tree to the Monument road on the right and go on to the Hidden Valley Campground.

Upon reaching Joshua Tree, phone the Monument headquarters, (714) 367-3444, and inquire about drinking water availability, especially if there is water in the spring at Ryan Campground (Ryan is two miles beyond Hidden Valley Campground, which has no water). If there is no water at Ryan Campground, enough water must be taken on in the town of Joshua Tree to last through dinner, breakfast, and the next day's trip across Pinto Basin, which can be very hot. If Ryan Spring is running, all that is needed is for dinner and breakfast in Hidden Valley Camp, unless you want to make the four-mile round trip to Ryan after you arrive in order to get water.

Day 2 — Hidden Valley Campground to Cottonwood Springs. Don't miss an early morning walking tour of Hidden Valley, a charming nature area and former rustlers' hideout. Continue by bike to Cap Rock. Turn right for a side trip to Salton View (climbing 1,000 feet in 6 miles); a 12-mile round trip. From Cap Rock turn left to Ryan Campground, and if water is available, take on at least one gallon plus bottles. Proceed to Belle Campground, then on to Cottonwood Springs, a total of 54 miles. From Belle to Cottonwood, the road drops down into Pinto Basin, a desolate area which can provide windblown sand. Here are located the Octillo Patch and Cholla Cactus Gardens.

Day 3 — Cottonwood Springs to Indio. A layover day at Cottonwood Springs is well worthwhile for hiking trips into the desert. Especially recommended is a trail (four miles each way) to the Lost Palms Oasis.

Leaving Cottonwood Springs, a short climb over a ridge leads to a 27-mile downhill breathtakingly beautiful ride through seas of wildflowers (in season) in Cottonwood Canyon and Shavers Valley. Coming out of the Monument, California Highway 195 is taken through Box Canyon, a water-sculptured gorge that suddenly opens out to a view of Salton Sea and the surrounding citrus groves. Here begins a very different experience through the dusty town of Mecca and 15 miles of California Highway 111 shoulder with heavy auto and truck traffic. One compensation is a date palm oasis on the left where there is shade and a restaurant serving date milkshakes and other goodies.

Notes

Carmel to San Luis Obispo, California

Location

California Highway 1 between Carmel and San Luis Obispo attracts cyclists for a variety of reasons. There is the scenic beauty of the Pacific coast, from redwoods to rocks to rolling hills. The winding road that drives motorists mad is a cycling delight. There are several side trip options including Pt. Lobos Reserve State Park (noted for its sea otter population) and the Hearst Castle at San Simeon.

There is Amtrak service in Salinas and you might consider starting your tour here if you have more time.

Season

Spring and fall are the best times of year to cycle this route. Try to avoid weekends and summer traffic. Winds are usually from the north. It can be foggy and damp any time of year in this area.

Accommodations

This can be made a combination camping and motel tour, or either one of the two. There are no motel accommodations between Big Sur and San Simeon.

Level of Difficulty

The Caltrans map describes the route south of Big Sur as demanding. There are some hills on the first day, but an early start and a moderate pace will get you to Kirk Creek Campground well before dark. We debated about going on to Plaskett Creek Campground (about five miles south of Kirk Creek) but the out-of-shape riders had gone far enough for one day. It was a good decision because passing Plaskett the next morning we discovered it was closed. It is advisable to check these things in advance.

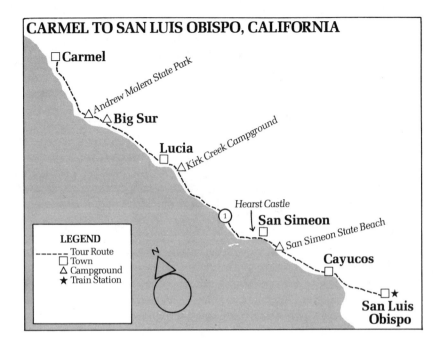

References

The Pacific Coast Bicentennial Route is available from Caltrans, 6002 Folsom Blvd., Sacramento, CA 95819. It is also available at many area bike shops. It is useful to have a street map of Monterey Peninsula and Monterey County.

Tour Outline and Points of Interest

Day 1. To exit Carmel, take Junipero Road which changes to Rio Road to the intersection with Highway 1. On your right you will pass the Carmel Mission, which was built in 1770. We breakfasted at this intersection before heading south.

At the intersection of Highway 1 and Rio Road, Pt. Lobos Reserve State Park entrance is on your right. This is a delightful side trip if you have the time.

Following Highway 1, Andrew Molera State Park is at mile 22. You next encounter Big Sur, where there are stores, water, and restrooms. This is a good place to buy snacks and food for lunch. Pfeiffer Big Sur State Park entrance will be on your left about 1½ miles down the road. On a longer trip, this might be a good place to camp overnight. There are few facilities between Big Sur and Cambria. It is advisable to stop at each gas station and store for water and supplies.

At mile 50 is Lucia, and five miles farther is Kirk Creek Campground. Bicycle sites are available. If you don't want to eat in camp, travel another four miles to Pacific Valley Center and a restaurant.

Day 2. Hearst Castle State Historical Monument is at approximately mile 91. Food is available at the entrance to the castle. There is also a store in the small town of San Simeon across Highway 1 west of the monument.

Next you will run into San Simeon State Beach and Campground. There are several stores, a motel, and restaurants here.

Day 3. Follow Ocean Boulevard to Cayucos. Return to Highway 1 and cycle to San Luis Obispo. You will have plenty of time to sightsee before catching an Amtrak train home.

Notes

Heart of the Mother Lode Tour

Location

The focus of this tour is scenic and historical. A number of Gold Rush towns and historical sites are along the 220-mile loop, including Fiddletown, which once had a Chinese population greater than San Francisco's Chinatown of that era. Scenic Daffodil Hill does justice to its name if visited in late March or early April.

San Francisco East Bay is the starting/ending point. However, while it can be readily cycled all the way by means of excellent routes, this tour utilizes train facilities so that the starting point is Pleasant Hill Bart Station, and the ending point is the Amtrak Station in Sacramento. This reduces the distance from 345 to 220 miles.

Pleasant Hill, the departure point, is a stop on the Bay Area Rapid Transit (BART) line, which makes it readily accessible from San Francisco and East Bay communities. Bicycles may be taken on the last car of the train during noncommute hours on weekdays, and during the operating day on weekends. For those not having permanent bike passes, a special one-ride pass will be issued by the station agent. Some of the stations have now been automated, and it may be necessary to gain access through a nonautomated station when a temporary pass is required.

Amtrak departs from the Southern Pacific Station in Sacramento daily at 1:30 P.M. Bicycles should be checked in at least one-half hour before departure. For reservations and information call (800) 648-3850. Arrival in Oakland is at 3:55 P.M.

Season

While this tour is below the snow line and could be cycled any time of the year, springtime provides the optimum of comfort and scenic beauty.

Accommodations

This tour uses a combination of motels and American Youth Hostels for overnight accommodations.

Level of Difficulty

This trip involves climbing from sea level to 2,500 feet elevation and descending again. Though the Mother Lode is noted for astounding hills, this route is designed so that it is within the range of most cyclists. It is important to ride the Mother Lode Exploration Loop (Day 2) in a clockwise direction, however, as Rams Horn Grade and Daffodil Hill are to be descended rather than climbed.

The heaviest flow of traffic will probably be on Route 49 which is utilized for two miles on the first day entering Jackson, and for nine miles on the exploration loop the second day.

References

A touring guide available for this area is *Bicycling Through the Mother Lode*, State Department of Parks and Recreation, P.O. Box 2390, Sacramento, CA 95811 ($1 plus postage).

Tour Outline and Points of Interest

Day 1 — Pleasant Hill to Jackson (1,000 feet) — 100 miles. Turn left onto Treat Boulevard which is adjacent to the Pleasant Hill Bart Station and go east on Treat Boulevard to Turtle Creek Road (signed bike route begins). Turn right on Turtle Creek Road to Ygnacio Valley Road, then left on Ygnacio Valley Road to Alberta Way, and right on Alberta Way a short distance to Pine Hollow Road. Next take a left on Pine Hollow Road to Clayton Road in the town of Clayton (last food and water stop for 35 miles).

Depart Clayton on Marsh Creek Road and proceed to Route 4. Turn right on Route 4 to Stockton (Highway 5 underpass). Continue east on Route 4 to Highway 99 crossing and onto Gillis Road (here marked Farmington). Take a left on Gillis Road to Main Street, right on Main Street to Jack Tone Road, left on Jack Tone Road to Comstock Road, right on Comstock Road to Clements Road, and left on Clements Road to the junction of Route 88. Turn right on Route 88/12 to Route 88 branching left. Remain on 88 to Martell where it joins 49 into Jackson.

By far the best of the motels in this area is the Country Squire. It is off the main traveled highway, is located by a running brook, and is walking distance from downtown and from the Kennedy Mine and its tailing wheels. It is shaded by a grove of trees and fronted

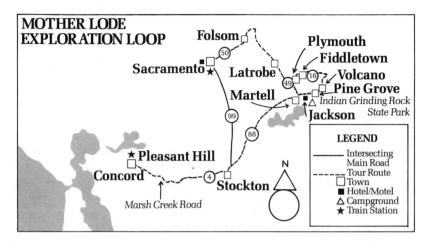

by a vast expanse of lawn. Hummingbirds abound, and cyclists are welcome. Those addicted to television are out of luck, however. Reservations are recommended by contacting the Country Squire Motel, 1105 N. Main St., Jackson, CA 95642. Phone (209) 223-1657.

Camping is available ten miles farther east at Indian Grinding Rock State Park by way of Route 88 and Pine Grove. Watch for the sign on the left as you pass through Pine Grove.

Day 2 — Heart of the Mother Lode Exploration Loop — 55 miles. North Main Street becomes Jackson Gate Road just beyond Country Squire Motel. Watch for the Kennedy Tailing Wheels signs on the right (well worth a walking side trip). Proceed to Highway 49/88. Turn right on 49/88 to Sutter Hill Road and right on Sutter Hill Road to Sutter Creek (explore walking bike). Continue north on 49 to Route 16. Turn right on Route 16 to Plymouth (again worth exploring), then right on Plymouth-Shenandoah Road and right again on Fiddletown-Silver Lake Road in approximately 0.5 mile. Continue to Fiddletown (watch for adobe Chinese historical monument on left).

Fiddletown to Lickwood Junction (2,500 feet elevation): Turn right (sharp) on Shake Ridge Road to Daffodil Hill, then a left on Rams Horn Grade to Volcano (walking tour recommended). Proceed through Volcano to Indian Grinding Rock State Park (includes a rather steep hill). Travel from Indian Grinding Rock State Park to Pine Grove via a left on Aqueduct Road (to avoid a short but impossibly steep hill on the more direct route), and then right on 88 to Pine Grove. Pine Grove to Jackson is downhill all the way.

Day 3 — Jackson to Sacramento — 65 miles. Depart Jackson

north as on day two by Route 49 to Route 16. Turn left on Route 16 to Latrobe Road, right on Latrobe Road, through Latrobe, El Dorado Hills and across Highway 50 to Green Valley Road. Take a left on Green Valley Road to Folsom (walking exploration of this Mother Lode historical town) and depart by way of Folsom Boulevard to Hazel. Go right on Hazel to the beginning point of the American River Bike Trail (south side), then left on the American River Bike Trail to South Side terminal point in C.M. Goethe Park. Turn left on the access road to Folsom Boulevard, right on La Riveria Drive to Watt Avenue. Turn right on Watt Avenue and cross bridge to the north side of American River and pick up the American River Bike Trail. Turn left on the Bike Trail to Old Sacramento.

Motels abound in Sacramento. A Best Western Motel is on the road from Discovery Park where the American River Bike Trail terminates in Old San Francisco. It is also a few blocks from the Southern Pacific Station.

An alternative for AYH members is the Youth Hostel located in the State Fairgrounds, whose access is by a branch bike route (right from the American River Bike Trail, with a clearly marked sign).

Notes

Sacramento River Tour

Location

This is a 214-mile tour from Davis to Redding, California, following the Sacramento River Route. The route given can just as easily be reversed. For easy access there are airports and bus stations in North Sacramento and Redding, and also Amtrak in Davis and Redding. However, the trains arrive and leave in the middle of the night, so be prepared. Tickets are cheaper for couples traveling together, and you must have reservations for this train.

Season

By far spring is the most spectacular time of year to cycle here, when the variety of orchards are blooming with wildflowers (March through April). Blossoms are staggered as each kind blooms only for about two weeks. Almonds are first (starting in late February), then plums and apricots, peaches and nectarines. Mid-March to late March, cherries are in bloom. Carry plenty of water, especially between Knights Landing and Meridian. Fall months would also be a pleasant time to visit the valley. Summer months are very hot and winter can be cold and rainy.

Accommodations

This can easily be taken as a motel or camping trip as there are several places for both along the route.

Level of Difficulty

The route follows the river as much as possible and therefore is basically flat on quiet back roads with very little traffic.

References

Use the California State Automobile Association maps for the Sacramento Valley Region and the Feather River Region. Caltrans also prints a guide for a more direct route, but there is infinitely more traffic.

If taking the side trip route through Woodland send for a color booklet, *Walking Tour of Historic Woodland,* to see restored Victorian homes and businesses. Available from Woodland City Hall, Woodland, CA 95695.

Tour Outline and Points of Interest

Day 1 — Davis to Colusa — 74 miles. Starting from the Amtrak station on 2nd Street, turn right on East Quad, then left on North Quad. Follow the bike route path which becomes Orchard Road, and then a bikepath over 113. Keep on a path parallel to Russell Boulevard. Take a right on County Road E7/98, another right on County Road 25A, and left again on County Road 99 into Woodland. Here you may take a side trip to visit the Victorian homes. Go right on Gibson, left on College, right on Cross Street, left on 2nd, left on Oak Avenue, right on College, right on Lincoln, left on 1st Street, and a right onto Main. Next turn left on 101 Road and pass under I-5. Turn right on 18C, then left on E8 to Knights Landing where services are available. Take the first left after crossing the bridge, which is Cranmore Road but is unmarked. Go left on Garmire Road, left on Meridian Road, left on Butte Slough Road, and left over the bridge into Colusa. Colusa has motels, stores and cafes, and also a camping area.

Day 2 — Colusa to Corning — 70 miles. Head back over the bridge from Colusa and go straight on River Road to the Princeton Ferry to cross the river. Proceed north on 45 to Hamilton City. If there's traffic, use the following route: right on Riz Road (Route 61) over the Sacramento River, left on Afton Boulevard, right on 50, left on Z, right on 48, left on Chico Butte City Highway, left on Ord Ferry Road, right on River Road, left on 32 into Hamilton City. Then proceed straight on Canal Road, left on Montgomery, and an immediate right then left becomes Cutter, right on 3rd, left on Moller, right on 4th, left on Clark, right on Capay, and right on Kirkwood into the town of Corning.

Day 3 — Corning to Redding — 70 miles. Cycle east on Main Street (A9) and take a left on Hall Street (the main road goes to the right; go straight about a block to the intersection with Dale, and then left on Hall). Turn right on All (Gyle Road) into Tehama which becomes 5th Street (bear left) and then San Benito Avenue. Go right on Holmes Road which becomes East Chard Avenue. Bear left. Turn

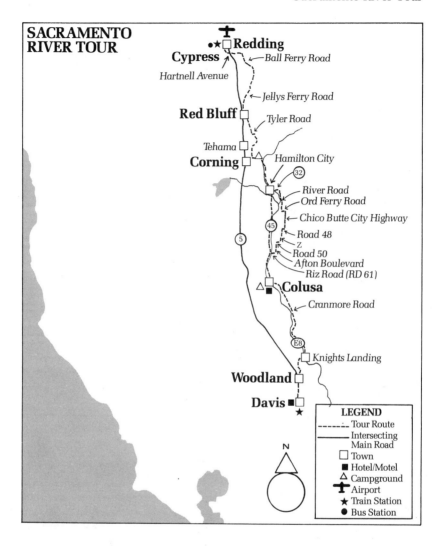

SACRAMENTO
RIVER TOUR

Redding
Cypress
—Ball Ferry Road
Hartnell Avenue
←Jellys Ferry Road
Red Bluff
Tyler Road
Tehama
Hamilton City
Corning
32
River Road
Ord Ferry Road
←Chico Butte City Highway
45
Road 48
5
z
Road 50
Afton Boulevard
Riz Road (RD 61)
Colusa
Cranmore Road
E8
Knights Landing
Woodland
Davis

LEGEND
- - - - - Tour Route
———— Intersecting Main Road
□ Town
■ Hotel/Motel
△ Campground
✝ Airport
★ Train Station
● Bus Station

N

right on Tyler Road and right on A8 into Red Bluff, where it becomes
Main Street. Turn right on Adobe to visit the Ide Adobe State Historical Park. Proceed on Main Street to I-5, then a right on Jellys
Ferry Road exit. Turn left on Ash Creek Road, which becomes Ball
Ferry Road. Stay to your right. Turn right on Deschutes Road, left
on Dersch, right on North Airport Road. Here you may encounter
heavy traffic and there are small shoulders. Go left on the unmarked
road after Rancho Road and before 44. Turn left on Hartnell Avenue,
right and left on Cypress, which is the main thoroughfare of Redding.

Notes

Rainbelt Tour—
Eugene, Oregon Loop

Location

A challenging route, this Eugene, Oregon, loop tour follows the McKenzie River Valley, crosses a volcanic grotesque wonderland at McKenzie Pass, 5,324 feet, and descends through a ponderosa pine forest to Sisters in central Oregon. Santiam Pass (4,817 feet) on the return trip lies between two heavily eroded volcanic remnants, Mt. Washington and Three-Fingered Jack.

Eugene, Oregon, is on the Amtrak line, and for those who wish to fly, there's Mahlon Sweet Airport.

Season

Route 242 of this tour is usually open from early July through October. Ask locally about road conditions. Route 242 over Mc-Kenzie Pass is not plowed and opens late.

Accommodations

Recommended campsites are beside the McKenzie River and on the shores of Suttle Lake. Come prepared for any kind of weather.

Level of Difficulty

Two hundred miles makes a pleasant three-day trip. Midweek is the best time to go, but watch for the bustling log trucks. Weekend traffic on 126 and 20 is heavy, but not unbearable. Prepare for a 10 + mile climb of McKenzie Pass. Make sure you have low gearing to creep up this switchback monster. Road surfaces are paved and of good to excellent quality.

References

Willamette National Forest and Deschutes National Forest maps

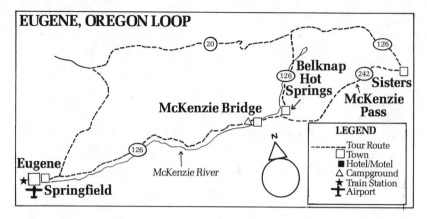

give detailed information about camping sites and roadside attractions. Forest Supervisor, P.O. Box 1060F, Eugene, OR 97401 (50¢); Eugene Area Bikeways Map, Public Works Dept., 858 Pearl St., Eugene, OR 97401 (free).

Tour Outline and Points of Interest

Day 1 — Eugene to McKenzie Bridge — 55 miles. Ask directions to the Eugene Bike Path that parallels the Willamette River. Once in adjoining Springfield, follow D Street to Mill Street. Go left on Mill to Centennial Boulevard, right on Centennial to 28th Street, and left on 28th to Marcola Road. Turn right on Marcola until you cross the McKenzie River at Hayden Bridge, then take a right on Camp Creek Road for approximately 10 miles until it flows into the McKenzie River Valley. Two excellent campsites near McKenzie Bridge are McKenzie Bridge Campground and Paradise Cove Campground.

Day 2 — McKenzie Bridge to Suttle Lake — 50 miles. Go east on Route 126 until you turn off onto 242 (McKenzie Pass Scenic Route). Cross McKenzie Pass to Sisters. From Sisters, ride northwest on Route 20 (or 126) to Suttle Lake.

Day 3 — Suttle Lake to Eugene — 95 miles. Travel west on 20 across Santiam Pass to 126 (Clear Lake cutoff). Take 126 to Camp Creek Road, then left on Marcola Road, left on 28th Street, right on Centennial Boulevard, left on Mill Street, and right on D Street to the Eugene Bike Path.

A possible stop on the return trip is Belknap Hot Springs, about 13 miles south of Clear Lake.

Notes